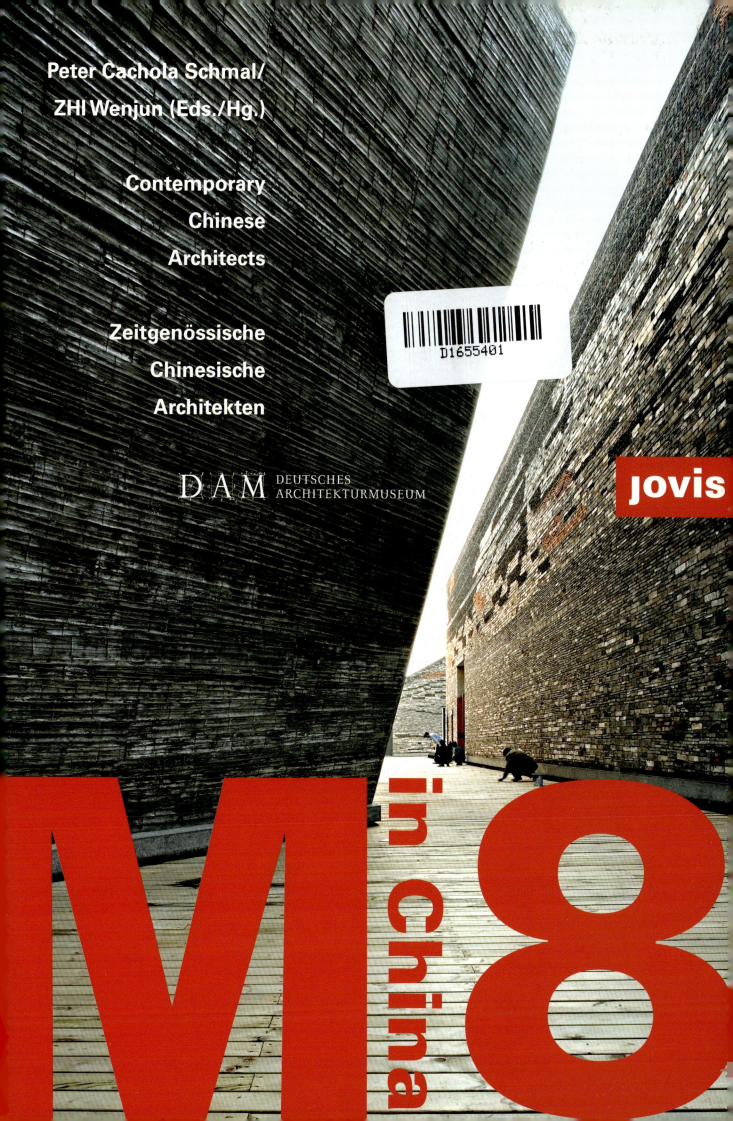

Contemporary
Chinese
Architects

Zeitgenössische
chinesische
Architekten

Peter Cachola Schmal/
ZHI Wenjun (Eds./Hg.)

DAM DEUTSCHES ARCHITEKTURMUSEUM

jovis

Contents Inhalt

Essays

Peter Cachola Schmal
   8 x Made in China   4
   8 x Made in China   6

ZHI Wenjun
   China under Sea Change   8
   China im Umbruch   10

Eduard Kögel
   From Material to Space   12
   Vom Material zum Raum   14

Robert Ivy
   Defining a Contemporary Chinese Architecture   16
   Definition einer zeitgenössischen chinesischen Architektur   18

Projects Projekte

Amateur Architecture Studio, Hangzhou   20
   Ceramic House, Jinhua City   22
   China Art Academy, New Campus of Xiangshan School, Hangzhou   26
   Ningbo History Museum, Ningbo   32

Atelier Z+, Shanghai   38
   Liantang Town Hall, Shanghai   40
   Building C, College of Architecture and Urban Planning, Tongji University, Shanghai   44
   Sino-French Center, Tongji University, Shanghai   50

DnA_Design and Architecture, Beijing   56
   Songzhuang Artists' Residence, Beijing   58
   Ordos Art Museum, Inner Mongolia   62
   Songzhuang Art Center, Beijing   68

Jiakun Architects, Chengdu   74
   Rebirth-brick Plan and HU Huishan Memorial, Sichuan   76
   Lu-ye-yuan Stone Sculpture Art Museum, Chengdu, Sichuan   78
   Museum of Cultural Revolution Clocks, Sichuan   84

MADA s.p.a.m., Shanghai	90
Guanghualu SOHO, Beijng	92
Xi'an Television and Broadcast Center, Xi'an	96
Jade Village (Well Hall, Father's House, Wine Dorm), Xi'an	100
standardarchitecture, Beijing	108
Qingcheng Mountain Stone Courtyard, Chengdu, Sichuan	110
Suzhou "AN" Club Tea House, Suzhou	114
Yaluntzangpu Boat Terminal, Linzhi, Tibet	120
Studio Pei-Zhu, Beijing	126
CAI Guoqiang Courtyard House Renovation, Beijing	128
Blur Hotel, Beijing	132
Publishing House, Beijing	138
TM Studio, Shanghai	142
ZHOU Chunya Art Studio, Shanghai	144
Park Block Renovation, Luqiao Old Town, Taizhou	148
Suquan Yuan, Shiquan Jie, Suzhou	154

8 x Made in China
Peter Cachola Schmal

Architect, Director German Architecture Museum (DAM) in Frankfurt/Main, critic and author

The Chinese architecture market is the most dynamic in the world; this is evident, for example, by the fact that according to information provided by *skyscrapercity* there are currently as many as forty-one "supertall towers" (over 300 meters high) under construction in China, in addition to the sixteen already standing. At 300 meters, the Commerzbank building by Foster and Partners (1998) once held the record for the tallest skyscraper in Europe. Contemporary private architecture is still something very new in China—private architectural practices have only been allowed since 1994. As such, until only recently foreign architects tended to look for joint-venture partners among one of over 10,000 state design institutes, the best known of which are ECADI (East China Architectural Design & Research Institute Co., Ltd) and SIADR (Shanghai Institute of Architectural Design and Research), each of which has more than 1,500 employees. We are, however, dedicating this publication and this exhibition project to the small flexibly operating practices, that win competitions, maintain international networks, appoint interns from around the world, and do precisely what sets their fellow architects worldwide apart: represent the labs that are developing architecture today. Under the umbrella of the Guest of Honor China at the 2009 International Book Fair and its motto "Tradition and Innovation" we have attempted to pinpoint new trends and emerging voices in Chinese architecture.

The head of the Chinese cultural program for the Book Fair, Mr. LIU Yongchun, Director of the Copyright Department of China National Publications Import and Export Corporation (CNPIEC), kindly forged links for us to the Shenyang publisher Liaoning Science and Technology Publishing House (LSTPH), and, despite the short lead-time, the collaboration has been very intensive and will hopefully bear further fruit. At this point I would like to express thanks in particular to YIN Qiang, the publishing house's project leader, and to Vice President of LSTPH, CHEN Ciliang, who were enormously enthusiastic in initiating this collaboration. In China, we also enjoyed the hospitality of the President, Mr. SONG Chunzi, and the General Manager of Liaoning Publishing Group, Ms. LIU Hong. YIN put us in contact with ZHI Wenjun, who is professor at Tongji University in Shanghai and Editor-in-Chief of the magazine *Shi Dai Jianzhu* (Time & Architecture). Together with XU Jie, he edited the outstanding book project *Contemporary Architecture in China 2004–2008,* and the present project draws strongly on its rich sources of information. Together with ZHI, we identified a group of eight young architecture practices that all stand out for their particularly sensitive treatment of material. We are delighted that all eight studios accepted the invitation and actively helped us with the preparations. This new generation of architects has a noticeably stronger relationship with the USA; after all, half of the heads of the eight practices selected studied in the USA and are still in contact with their former fellow students. On the other hand, there is also a lot of interest in Chinese architecture from abroad. Eduard Kögel from Berlin is the editor of the only Internet platform for Chinese architecture (chinese-architects.com) and, together with Ulf Meyer, curated the first exhibition on young Chinese architecture outside of China, in 2001 at the Berlin-based gallery Aedes. He formulates his findings from following trends over the past five years. I am also delighted that chinese-architects.com is supporting our *M8 in China* project as a media partner. I would very much like to thank Mario Lorenz, the designer from deserve in Wiesbaden for his work for DAM.

The eight architects selected
I was familiar with WANG Shu and LU Wenyu of **Amateur Architects** in Hangzhou (founded in 1998) from the 2006 Architecture Biennial in Venice, where they captivated visitors with their installation comprising thousands of reused roof tiles. Their buildings delivered everything this installation promised. With its monumental fortress-like collage of bricks, their most recent construction, the History Museum in Ningbo (p.32), demonstrates that the couple indeed numbers among the most forceful voices in the country. In my view, the same applies with regard to Beijing architects **standardarchitecture,** which was founded in 2002, and three of whose partners studied at Harvard. Their projects in Linzhi, Tibet, are perfectly integrated into the context with their loving use of materials, and they touch me greatly. The subtle ferry mooring on the Yaluntzangpu River (p.120) and the Namchabawa Visitor Center in particular are masterly projects that link regional details, choice of material, and sculptural restraint with current spatial usage to the highest of standards. **Jiakun Architects** from Chengdu in Sichuan (founded in 1999) caught the eye at the last Architecture Biennial in Venice in 2008, when their tile research formed part of the Chinese presentation in the remote gardens of the Arsenale. Using straw and broken bricks recovered from the rubble of the Great Sichuan Earthquake on May 12, 2008 they created a new brick, which not only offers advantages in terms of price, but through the integrated straw fibers possesses sufficient tensile strength to be used for construction in earthquake areas. TONG Ming, who founded his **TM Studio** in 2000, on the other hand, is a loner, who alongside his position as professor at Tongji University in Shanghai works on small projects. His work is characterized by a remarkable devotion to detail, as demonstrated by the slender, shady Suquan Yuan Tea House in Suzhou (p.154), which is intended to draw attention to itself as the entrance to a settlement that is still to be developed. For the most part, the moniker Tea House indicates that an edifice had to be designed with no specific layout in mind, as all Chinese architects know from experience. The Faculty of Architecture at Tongji University was designed by the local firm **Atelier Z+** in Shanghai (founded in 2002). ZHANG Bin, who also studied in Paris, and his partner ZHOU Wei have rendered outstanding services to their university and have constructed a spatially complex and diverse stand-alone for the School of Architecture and Urban Planning, where tomorrow's architects can study spatial contexts daily (p.44). The architect in the group best known in the West, MA Qingyun, who studied at the University of Pennsylvania, com-

mutes professionally between East and West. Following years as a visiting professor worldwide, he is now Dean of the Department of Architecture at the University of Southern California in Los Angeles. The works produced by his Shanghai practice **MADA s.p.a.m.** (founded in 1996) are repeatedly a source of amazement on account of their diversity and stylistic confidence. In addition to the fancy administration building for SOHO, one of the most extravagant project developers in China (p.92), one can also see traditional masonry, as in the Jade Village project (p.100). ZHU Pei earned his Master's at the University of California in Berkeley and his Beijing **Studio Pei-Zhu** is also well known in the West. On display are his metropolitan conversions such as the Blur Hotel in Beijing, with a concentrated matrix of rooms behind translucent façades (p.132), and the studio for artist CAI Guoqiang in a former *huton*, which could well initiate a change in trend for this type of building, which has all but become extinct (p.128). The only studio to be run entirely by a female architect is **DnA_Design and Architecture** in Beijing, which was founded in 2004. As one of her first projects, XU Tiantian, who also studied at Harvard, created the Ordos Art Museum, a topographical study in Inner Mongolia (p.62). The design of her cluster-like Songzhuang Artists' Residence is just as spatially complex, and the first tenants are just moving in (p.58).

In the future, we will undoubtedly hear a lot about her, as indeed about the other practices in this selection. With their attention to regional typology, to the unique character of the specific local context, and their frequent rediscovery of traditional rural craftsmen's techniques they have an advantage over the giant architectural factories of the design institutes I mentioned at the outset, and which, in partnership with just about all the world's major companies, construct spectacular, gigantic buildings in all big Chinese cities, for the most part without considering even a regional touch. In the foreseeable future these young Chinese architecture practices will extend their reach and provide high-quality, self-confident Chinese architecture internationally, and I feel certain they will be invited to take part in high-prestige international competitions. Following a wave of exports to China since the mid-1990s, we will then witness the first imports of architecture "Made in China" here. I am already looking forward to it.

8 x Made in China
Peter Cachola Schmal

Architekt, Direktor des Deutschen Architekturmuseums
(DAM) in Frankfurt am Main, Architekturkritiker und -autor

Der chinesische Architekturmarkt ist der dynamischste der Welt. Das ist zum Beispiel daran zu erkennen, dass nach Angaben von *skyscrapercity* derzeit allein 41 „supertall towers" (Definition: über 300 Meter Höhe) in China im Bau sind, zusätzlich zu den 16 bereits existierenden. 300 Meter – das war einmal der Höhenrekord der Frankfurter Commerzbank von Foster and Partners 1998, als sie mit dieser Marke noch den Rang des höchsten Wolkenkratzers Europas besetzen konnten. Gleichwohl ist zeitgenössische private Architekturpraxis noch recht neu in China – erst seit 1994 ist die Gründung privater Architekturbüros erlaubt. Vor gar nicht langer Zeit landeten ausländische Architekten auf der Suche nach einem Joint-Venture-Partner daher bei einem der über 10.000 staatlichen Designinstitute. Die bekanntesten unter ihnen sind ECADI (East China Architectural Design & Research Institute Co., Ltd) und SIA-DR (Shanghai Institute of Architectural Design and Research) mit ihren jeweils über 1500 Mitarbeitern. Wir widmen diese Publikation und dieses Ausstellungsprojekt allerdings den kleinen, flexibel agierenden Büros, die sich in Wettbewerben behaupten, internationale Netzwerke pflegen und Praktikanten aus aller Welt einstellen und eben das tun, was ihre Kollegen weltweit auszeichnet, nämlich das eigentliche Entwicklungslabor der Architektur darstellen. Unter dem Schirm des Gastlandes China der Internationalen Buchmesse 2009 und dessen Motto „Tradition und Innovation" haben wir versucht, neue Tendenzen und aufkommende Stimmen in der chinesischen Architektur aufzuspüren.

Dank der Vermittlung des Leiters des chinesischen Kulturprogramms zur Buchmesse, Herrn LIU Yongchun, Direktor des Copyright Department of China National Publications Import and Export Corporation (CNPIEC), zum Shenyanger Verlag Liaoning Science and Technology Publishing House (LSTPH) entstand eine Kooperation, die trotz der Kürze der Zeit sehr intensiv war und hoffentlich noch viele weitere Früchte tragen wird. An dieser Stelle sei besonders der Projektleiterin des Verlags, YIN Qian, und dem Vize-Präsidenten von LSTPH, CHEN Ciliang, gedankt, die diese Kooperation mit viel Begeisterung realisierten. Vor Ort genossen wir auch die Gastfreundschaft des Präsidenten, Herrn SONG Chunzi, und der General Managerin der Liaoning Publishing Group, Frau LIU Hong. YIN verknüpfte uns mit dem Shanghaier Professor der Tongji University und Chefredakteur der Zeitschrift *Shi Dai Jianzhu* („Time & Architecture"), ZHI Wenjun. Er hatte, zusammen mit XU Jie, das hervorragende Buchprojekt *Contemporary Architecture in China 2004–2008* herausgebracht, auf dessen reichhaltige Informationsbasis sich die Auswahl für dieses Projekt stützt. Zusammen mit ZHI bestimmten wir eine Gruppe von acht aufstrebenden Architekturbüros, denen in meinen Augen ein besonders sensibler Umgang mit Material zu eigen ist. Wir freuen uns, dass alle acht Büros die Einladung angenommen haben und uns tatkräftig bei der Vorbereitung unterstützt haben.

Der USA-Bezug dieser nächsten Architektengeneration ist erkennbar groß, immerhin haben die Hälfte der Inhaber der acht ausgewählten Büros in den USA studiert und halten enge Kontakte zu ihren Kommilitonen. Auch von außen gibt es ein großes Interesse an der chinesischen Architektur. Eduard Kögel aus Berlin, Redakteur der einzigen Internet-Plattform zu chinesischer Architektur (chinese-architects.com) kuratierte 2001 mit Ulf Meyer die erste Ausstellung über junge chinesische Architekten außerhalb Chinas in der Berliner Galerie Aedes. Er formuliert seine Erkenntnisse aus der Beobachtung der Entwicklung der letzten Jahre. Ich freue mich auch, dass chinese-architects.com als Medienpartner unser Projekt *M8 in China* unterstützt. Für die Arbeit im DAM möchte ich mich recht herzlich bei Mario Lorenz, dem Designer von deserve aus Wiesbaden, bedanken.

Die ausgewählten acht Architekten
WANG Shu und LU Wenyu von **Amateur Architects** aus Hangzhou (gegr. 1998) waren mir von der Architekturbiennale in Venedig 2006 bekannt, wo sie mit ihrer Installation aus Tausenden wiederverwendeter Dachziegel die Szene entzückten. Ihre Bauten lösten alles ein, was diese Installation versprach. Auch ihr neuestes Werk, das History Museum in Ningbo mit seiner monumentalen festungsartigen Collage von Mauerziegeln (S. 32) zeigt, dass das Paar zu den stärksten Stimmen des Landes gezählt werden muss. Ähnlich ergeht es mir mit **standardarchitecture** aus Peking(gegr. 2002, drei der vier Partner sind in Harvard ausgebildet), deren ganz natürlich in den Kontext eingefügte Projekte in Linzhi (Tibet) mit ihrer liebevollen Materialisierung mich sehr berühren. Besonders die feine Fähranlegerstelle am Fluss Yaluntzangpu (S. 120) und das Namchabawa Visitor Center sind meisterhafte Projekte mit einer Verknüpfung von regionaler Detaillierung und Materialauswahl sowie skulpturaler Zurückhaltung mit aktueller Raumdisposition auf höchstem Niveau. **Jiakun Architects** aus Chengdu/Sichuan (gegr. 1999) fielen auf der letzten Architekturbiennale Venedig 2008 auf, als sie mit ihren Ziegelforschungen Teil der chinesischen Präsentation im entlegenen Garten des Arsenale waren. Aus Stroh und Bruchziegeln, welche aus dem Schutt des Großen Erdbebens von Sichuan vom 12. Mai 2008 stammten, fertigten sie ein neues Ziegelprodukt, das nicht nur vom Preis her vorteilhaft ist, sondern durch die eingewirkten Strohfasern genügend Zugfestigkeit für das Bauen in Erdbebengebieten bietet. TONG Ming ist dagegen ein Einzelgänger (Bürogründung **TM Studio** 2000), der neben seiner Stelle als Professor an der Shanghaier Tongji University kleinere Projekte realisiert, mit einer bewundernswerten Hingabe zum Detail, wie das schmale schattendurchwirkte Tea House Suquan Yuan in Suzhou (S. 154), das als Auftakt einer noch zu entwickelnden Siedlung auf sich aufmerksam machen soll. Der Begriff Tea House weist meist darauf hin, dass ein Bauwerk ohne konkretes Raumprogramm geplant werden musste, wie alle chinesischen Architekten aus Erfahrung wissen. Die Architekturfakultät der Tongji Universität (S. 44) stammt vom örtlichen Büro **Atelier Z+** aus Shanghai (gegr. 2002). ZHANG Bin (Studium unter anderem in Paris) und seine Partnerin ZHOU Wei haben sich um ihre Universität verdient gemacht und der Schule für Architektur und Stadtplanung

ein räumlich komplexes und vielschichtiges Einzelbauwerk errichtet, wo die Architekten von morgen täglich die Kunst räumlicher Zusammenhänge studieren können. Der im Westen bekannteste Architekt innerhalb dieser Gruppe, MA Qingyun (Ausbildung an der University of Pennsylvania), pendelt beruflich zwischen Ost und West, da er als Dean den Architekturfachbereich der University of Southern California in Los Angeles leitet, nach Jahren als Gastprofessor weltweit. Die Arbeiten seines Shanghaier Büros **MADA s.p.a.m.** (gegr. 1996) verblüffen immer wieder durch stilsichere Vielfältigkeit. Neben dem ausgefallenen Verwaltungsbau für SOHO, einen der extravagantesten Projektentwickler in China, (S. 92) sieht man auch traditionelles Maurerhandwerk wie beim Projekt Jade Village (S. 100). An der UC Berkeley hat ZHU Pei seinen Master gemacht, sein Pekinger Büro **Studio Pei-Zhu** ist im Westen ebenfalls bereits bekannter. Seine metropolitanen Umbauten werden ausgestellt, wie das Pekinger Blur Hotel mit einer dichten Matrix an Räumen hinter transluzenten Fassaden (S. 132) oder das Studio für den Künstler CAI Guoqiang in einem ehemaligen hutong, das eine Trendwende für diese fast komplett ausgelöschte Typologie einleiten könnte (S. 128). Das einzige allein von einer Frau geleitete Büro ist das erst 2004 gegründete **DnA_Design and Architecture** in Peking. XU Tiantian, die ebenfalls in Harvard ausgebildet ist, hat als eines ihrer ersten Projekte eine topografische Studie in der inneren Mongolei gebaut, das Ordos Art Museum (S. 62). Ihr clusterartiges Wohngebilde Songzhuang Artists' Residence (S. 58) ist ebenso räumlich komplex gedacht und wird gerade bezogen.

Wir werden sicher in der Zukunft noch viel von ihr hören, wie auch von den anderen Büros dieser Auswahl. Denn sie können sich mit ihrer Hinwendung zur regionalen Typologie, zur Einzigartigkeit des ortsspezifischen Kontexts und mit der Wiederentdeckung der traditionellen Handwerkstechniken auf dem Lande einen Vorsprung gegenüber den zu Anfang erwähnten riesigen Architekturfabriken der Designinstitute verschaffen, die in Partnerschaft mit so ziemlich allen größeren Büros der Welt spektakuläre und gigantische Bauten in allen chinesischen Millionenstädten errichten, meist ohne besondere Rücksicht auf einen regionalen Bezug. In absehbarer Zeit werden diese jungen chinesischen Architekturbüros ihren Radius erweitern und qualitativ hochwertige sowie selbstbewusst chinesische Architektur international anbieten, und sie werden zu prestigeträchtigen, internationalen Wettbewerben eingeladen werden. Nach einer Welle von Architekturexporten ins Reich der Mitte seit den 1990er Jahren werden wir dann die ersten Architekturimporte „made in China" erleben, hier bei uns. Ich freue mich schon darauf.

China under Sea Change
Chinese Contemporary Architecture amid Globalization

ZHI Wenjun

Architect, Editor-in-Chief of *Time + Architecture* magazine, Professor of the College of Architecture and Urban Planning, Tongji University, Shanghai

Today, a discussion on architecture of any kind has to touch on the concept of globalization. Since opening up to the world in the 1980s, every aspect of contemporary Chinese society has been increasingly influenced by the forces of globalization. This is particularly true with architecture, a cultural field. Partly due to the lack of communication with the rest of the world in the recent past, Chinese contemporary architects sometimes copied Western styles or misinterpreted Western concepts, without a careful consideration of the local contexts. On the other hand, architectural theory and history produced in the West have not shown much attention to Chinese contemporary architecture for most of the twentieth century. With the fast developments in Chinese economy and culture in the recent decades, however, many Chinese architects have started to search for regional characteristics, calling for a mix of modernity with local identities. A number of brave experiments in constructed works have appeared. Meanwhile, Western scholars have shown growing interest in Chinese contemporary architecture, ignited by the rapid developments in the built environment of Chinese cities. The two forces—one from the inside of China and the other from the outside—are reshaping Chinese contemporary architecture.

The Western Model and China
With the current globalization primarily based on the Western system of values, it is no wonder that Western culture has dominated the world architectural scene. If we look back at the history of Chinese modern architecture, we will find that it has consciously or unconsciously followed Western Modernism. We Chinese architects and critics judge our own works with Western criteria. At the same time, Western observers' evaluation of Chinese contemporary architecture has not been completely objective either. Based on Western standards, these critics and reporters tend to focus on a few projects with construction qualities comparable to a building in Europe or North America, while neglecting the large amount of "average" buildings emerging daily in the built environment of China. These observers tend to chase after exotic "Chinese" features or "modern" designs that only reflect their own desires. Such limited perspectives have prevented Westerners from truly understanding China.
We need to recognize that architectural development in China differs from that in the West of any historical period. In particular, Chinese building industry demands a much shorter time period to realize a project. The socioeconomic environment is far more complex and ever changing, with nothing remaining permanent in today's reform era. In the past twenty years, many Chinese architects have acknowledged and understood this complexity and contradiction in contemporary Chinese society. They have avoided blindly following Western models. In addition, they have attempted to develop individualized strategies to respond to the unique social, political, economic, and cultural realities. Rather than a compromise, such practical wisdom represents a balance maintained between architectural ideas and ideals and the harsh real world.

The Problems of Contemporary Chinese Architecture
China has achieved rapid growth in the past two decades. Nevertheless, the Chinese society as a whole still remains in the early stages of industrialization and urbanization, with limited material wealth. The production of space and aesthetic forms aims chiefly at maximizing profits with minimum costs. Developers tend to pursue larger quantity and scale of projects and faster construction speed, causing rapid urban expansion. Various architectural styles and urban planning models have been put to use within a short time span in Chinese cities, causing environmental homogeneity in some areas and fragmentation in others. Meanwhile, the widespread anxiety over the lack of one's own identity has pushed architects to fervently search for whatever is new and popular. The fashion-like places created in such a process are often being duplicated in other sites right away. Primarily relying on fragmentary and simultaneous transportation of ideas from Western cultures, many Chinese contemporary architectural works lost touch with local contexts and failed to establish connections with the history and culture of the community. Being the manufacturers of commodities, Chinese architects have no way to escape from the continuing process of producing profits for capital. As the bearers of cultural ideals, Chinese architects find little support to search architectural languages appropriate for today's China, given the rapid modernization and the breaking of tradition. Chinese architects see themselves in a dilemma.

Search for Our Own Answers
As the largest developing country in the world, China has a huge population, poor infrastructure, and uneven states of modernization among its different regions. In terms of both scale and complexity, the challenges China encounters in its development are unprecedented in the world. The great earthquake on May 12, 2008 in the Sichuan Province of China revealed the gravity of problems hidden in Chinese society. Many scholars at home and abroad have reached the conclusion that one cannot use Western standards to evaluate the development of China. Rather, the unique local conditions must be taken into consideration.
Such an insight demands that Chinese architects and scholars shift their focus to the particular time and place of their projects. They need to understand better the history and tradition related to a project. But more importantly, they need to pay attention to the unique details of current daily life on the site and corresponding design solutions. In addition, Chinese architectural professionals must develop a resistance to pressures from both commercial and political interests, maintaining their integrity in both technical and aesthetic aspects of design. The good news is that, in recent years, some Chinese architects have started the switching from a "heroic" approach to a "bottom-up" one, devoting their major

efforts to local social issues, construction methods, and building materials. This new trend has brought us much hope.

The Selection of Architects and Their Works
The books twenty-four works by eight selected architects are the complete creative and influential works in contemporary China. Most of these architectures are outstanding experimental design works by fourth-generation architects, showcasing their understanding and innovative response to local history, culture, and current realities. These works offer a kind of global view on Chinese problems, and these architects attempt to make Chinese architecture consistent with international strategy and policy. We will witness the transformation of contemporary Chinese architecture through these works.

Selection Keyword: Non-mainstream and Unique
In China, large-scale design institutes are still playing the leading role, but the eight architects and studios selected here represent individuals, hence their design works are not the products of large-scale design institutes. Their architectural works are only a very small part of the building projects in China—the special cases outside the system. They are exploring new ways for Chinese architecture within the context of globalization, and they are finding the answers. Their efforts, as well as their approaches, offer views of the reality of Chinese contemporary architecture.

Educational Background Keyword: Local and International
Almost all of the architects in the exhibition have received higher professional education; for instance, TONG Ming and WANG Shu are Doctors of Architecture. Some of them studied only in China, while others began their education in China and then studied and worked abroad for years. Those with educational and work experiences abroad are not only well aware of developments in international construction, but frequently participate in academic exchanges at home and internationally.

Design Keyword: Research and Practice
The design work of all of the architects (studios) in this book is research-oriented and full of experimental significance, even though most of them are small projects. Some of these architects also teach, and their research achievements are reflected in their design work. Therefore, in comparison with other Chinese architecture, their architectural concepts are more novel in terms of their characteristics and approach.

Career Keyword: Small-scale Office and Studio
Since the 1990s, private architectural studios in China have developed gradually, with more and more young architects establishing their own design companies. With the exception of large state-run design institutes, the influence of private architectural firms has grown significantly. These firms were established during the era of large-scale construction, which created more opportunities for architects to gain experience and implement their own creative ideas.

Architectural Works Keyword: Small-scale and Urban Fringe
Most of the architectural works selected for the exhibition are small-scale public buildings, which provide architects space to imagine and create. Public buildings are not as limited with regard to design restrictions as residential construction, which has rigorous requirements related to sunlight and functional requirements, etc. While a few of these works are located in the commercial center of the city, others are located at the urban fringes or in special cultural and educational areas. In these areas, projects were less constrained by commercial interests, providing more creative freedom.

Conclusion: "Chinese Characteristics?"
In the past three decades, China has accomplished vast economic and social progress. Through trial and error, people have concluded that it is both possible and necessary to adopt "an approach with Chinese characteristics." The Chinese experiment is making a unique contribution to world civilization, which has been dominated by the Western model alone for so long. Today, the "Chinese characteristics" in economic development are waiting for future tests, including the ongoing global economic crisis. But in the field of architecture, we have to ask the following questions: Does the physical landscape of new Chinese buildings and cities present a good architectural interpretation of the "Chinese model?" Is there any universal implication in the Chinese architectural experiments? How much cultural confidence can Chinese contemporary architecture give us?

China im Umbruch
Zeitgenössische chinesische
Architektur im Kontext der
Globalisierung

Von Zhi Wenjun

Architekt, Chefredakteur des Magazins *Time + Architecture*,
Professor am College of Architecture and Urban Planning,
Tongji University, Shanghai

Heutzutage kommt keine Diskussion über Architektur am Thema der Globalisierung vorbei. Und auch die moderne chinesische Gesellschaft ist seit der Öffnungspolitik der 1980er Jahre zunehmend den Kräften der Globalisierung ausgesetzt. Dies wird insbesondere im Bereich der Architektur sichtbar. Aufgrund des fehlenden Austausches mit dem Rest der Welt in der jüngeren Vergangenheit kopierten chinesische Architekten teilweise westliche Stile oder missverstanden westliche Ideen, ohne lokale Zusammenhänge zu beachten. Andererseits haben weder die Architekturtheorie noch die Architekturgeschichte des Westens der zeitgenössischen chinesischen Architektur im 20. Jahrhundert besondere Beachtung geschenkt. Aber mit der rasanten wirtschaftlichen und kulturellen Entwicklung Chinas in den letzten Jahrzehnten haben sich viele chinesische Architekten einer Integration von Moderne und lokaler Identität zugewandt und regionale Eigenheiten für ihre Architektur neu entdeckt.

Mittlerweile sind eine Anzahl mutiger baulicher Experimente tatsächlich umgesetzt worden. Und im Westen steigt – schon wegen des explosionsartigen Wachstums der Städte – das Interesse an chinesischer zeitgenössischer Architektur. Beide Kräfte – die von innerhalb und die von außerhalb Chinas – verändern die zeitgenössische chinesische Architektur auf nachhaltige Weise.

China und das westliche Vorbild
Da der gegenwärtige Globalisierungsprozess vorrangig vom westlichen Wertesystem getragen wird, verwundert es kaum, dass die westliche Kultur die globale Architekturszene beherrscht. Und die Geschichte der modernen chinesischen Architektur ist, bewusst oder unbewusst, der westlichen Moderne gefolgt. Selbst wir chinesischen Architekten und Kritiker beurteilen unsere eigenen Arbeiten nach westlichen Kriterien. Gleichzeitig aber ist die Einschätzung chinesischer zeitgenössischer Architektur durch westliche Beobachter nie ganz objektiv gewesen. Der Blick der Kritiker und Journalisten konzentriert sich nahezu ausschließlich auf die wenigen Projekte, die eine vergleichbare bauliche Qualität wie in Europa oder Nordamerika aufweisen; die Mehrheit des „durchschnittlichen", tagtäglichen Baugeschehens in China bleibt unbeachtet. Fast alle Beobachter jagen exotischen „chinesischen" Eigenarten hinterher oder wollen „moderne" Entwürfe aufspüren, die eher ihren eigenen Vorstellungen entsprechen. Aber aus einer so verengten Perspektive lässt sich China nicht wirklich begreifen.

Es ist wichtig zu verstehen, dass sich die architektonische Entwicklung in China, gleich welcher Epoche, von der architektonischen Entwicklung in der westlichen Welt unterscheidet. Insbesondere die Realisierungszeit von Bauten ist in der chinesischen Bauwirtschaft kürzer, die sozioökonomische Umgebung ist ungleich komplexer und fortwährenden Änderungen unterworfen – nichts bleibt in der heutigen Zeit der Umwälzungen langfristig bestehen. In den vergangenen 20 Jahren haben viele chinesische Architekten jene Komplexität und Widersprüchlichkeit ihrer heutigen Gesellschaft erkannt und verstanden. Sie folgen nicht mehr blind den westlichen Vorbildern, sondern versuchen, individuelle Strategien zur Lösung spezifischer sozialer, politischer, ökonomischer und kultureller Probleme zu entwickeln. Diese Art praktischer Weisheit ist kein Kompromiss, sondern die Balance zwischen architektonischen Idealen und der rauen Wirklichkeit.

Die Probleme zeitgenössischer chinesischer Architektur
China hat sich in den vergangenen zwei Jahrzehnten rapide gewandelt. Dennoch befindet sich die chinesische Gesellschaft als Ganzes immer noch im Anfangsstadium der Industrialisierung und Urbanisierung und verfügt nur über begrenzten materiellen Wohlstand. Die Produktion von Raum und ästhetischen Formen zielt vorrangig auf eine Profitmaximierung bei gleichzeitiger Kostenminimierung. Projektentwickler verfolgen immer mehr und immer größere Projekte, die in immer kürzerer Zeit realisiert werden müssen. Dadurch dehnen sich die Städte rasant aus. Innerhalb kurzer Zeit kamen dabei eine Vielzahl architektonischer Stile und städtebaulicher Modelle zum Einsatz. Die Folgen: Eintönigkeit auf der einen Seite, Fragmentierung auf der anderen. Vor allem die weitverbreitete Angst vor einem Mangel an eigener Identität zwang die Architekten immer wieder zur fieberhaften Suche nach Neuem und Populärem. Die modischen Ergebnisse dieses Prozesses werden woanders oft umgehend kopiert. Da sie aber hauptsächlich auf der bloßen zusammenhangslosen Übertragung westlicher Ideen beruhen, haben zahllose zeitgenössische chinesische Bauten ihre Beziehung zum lokalen Kontext verloren und keinerlei Verbindung mehr zur jeweiligen Geschichte oder Kultur.

Mit ihren Bauten stellen die chinesischen Architekten im Grunde Konsumgüter her und werden damit ein Teil des andauernden Prozesses der Mehrwertproduktion für das Kapital. Die angestammte Rolle der Architekten als Träger kultureller Ideale gerät in Vergessenheit; chinesische Architekten, die nach einem angemessenen architektonischen Ausdruck für das heutige China im Angesicht von rasender Modernisierung und dem Bruch mit der Tradition suchen, finden kaum Unterstützung. In diesem Sinne befindet sich die Architektur in China in einem Dilemma.

Die Suche nach eigenen Antworten
Mit seiner enormen Bevölkerungszahl, einer schwachen Infrastruktur und je nach Region höchst unterschiedlichem Modernisierungsgrad ist China das größte Entwicklungsland der Welt. Die Herausforderungen, denen sich China in seiner Entwicklung gegenüber sieht, sind in Ausmaß und Komplexität bisher in der Welt beispiellos. Das große Erdbeben vom 12. Mai 2008 in Sichuan zeigte, wie schwerwiegend die verborgenen Probleme der chinesischen Gesellschaft sind. Viele Intellektuelle im In- und Ausland kamen zu der Überzeugung, dass man die Entwicklung Chinas nicht nach westlichen Maßstäben messen darf. Vielmehr müssen die spezifischen örtlichen Gegebenheiten besondere Berücksichtigung finden.

Diese Einsicht fordert auch die chinesischen Architekten und Akademiker: Sie müssen dem konkreten Ort und Zeitpunkt ihrer Projekte endlich mehr Aufmerksamkeit schenken. Sie müssen die Geschichte und Tradition, die mit den Projekten verknüpft sind, besser verstehen. Sie müssen das Leben vor Ort im Detail beobachten und die Erkenntnisse in ihre Entwürfe einfließen lassen. Darüber hinaus sollten chinesische Architekten dem Druck kommerzieller und politischer Interessen durchaus Paroli bieten und ihre Integrität als Entwerfer in technischer und ästhetischer Hinsicht aufrechterhalten. Erfreulich ist, dass sich in den letzten Jahren einige chinesische Architekten von einem eher „heroischen" Ansatz abgewandt haben und ihr Hauptaugenmerk heute auf lokale und soziale Belange, Bauweisen und Baumaterialien gerichtet haben: Das macht uns große Hoffnung.

Die Auswahl der Architekten und ihrer Werke
Die in diesem Buch präsentierten 24 Beiträge von acht ausgewählten Architekten sind eine umfassende Werkschau kreativer und einflussreicher Arbeiten im heutigen China. Die meisten dieser Bauten sind herausragende experimentelle Entwürfe von Architekten der vierten Generation, die demonstrieren, wie das Verständnis der örtlichen Geschichte und Kultur und aktueller Probleme zu innovativen Lösungen führt. Fast alle Arbeiten bieten eine umfassende Perspektive auf chinesische Eigenheiten und zeigen, wie die ausgewählten Architekten versuchen, die moderne chinesische Architektur in die internationalen Debatten und Ausrichtungen zu integrieren. Anhand der gezeigten Arbeiten lässt sich die Transformation zeitgenössischer chinesischer Architektur nachvollziehen.

Auswahlkriterien: Einzigartigkeit und Unangepasstheit
In China geben die großen Designinstitute immer noch den Ton an. Alle hier ausgewählten Architekten und Büros agieren jedoch unabhängig. Ihre Arbeiten sind nicht die der Institute. Ihr architektonisches Schaffen bildet nur einen sehr kleinen Teil der Bautätigkeit Chinas – sozusagen eine Ausnahme. Sie suchen im Kontext der Globalisierung nach neuen Wegen in der chinesischen Architektur und finden Antworten. Ihr Engagement und ihre Arbeitsweisen öffnen den Blick auf das reale aktuelle Baugeschehen in China.

Lokaler und internationaler Bildungshintergrund
Nahezu alle vorgestellten Architekten haben ein architektonisches Hochschulstudium absolviert. TONG Ming und WANG Shu besitzen sogar einen Doktor in Architektur. Einige von ihnen studierten nur in China, andere haben viele Jahre im Ausland studiert und gearbeitet. Diejenigen mit Arbeits- und Studienerfahrungen im Ausland sind sich nicht nur der Entwicklungen der internationalen Bauindustrie bewusst, sondern nehmen auch regelmäßig am nationalen und internationalen akademischen Austausch teil.

Forschung und Praxis
Die Entwurfsarbeit aller gezeigten Büros ist analytischer Natur und voller experimenteller Ansätze, obwohl es sich bei den meisten Projekten um kleinere Arbeiten handelt. Manche der Architekten gehen einer Lehrtätigkeit nach, sodass sich eigene Forschungsergebnisse in ihren Arbeiten widerspiegeln. Diese architektonischen Konzepte zeichnen sich daher durch besondere Innovation aus.

Berufliche Perspektiven in kleinen Büros
Seit 1990 haben sich in China zunehmend private Architekturbüros gegründet, mehr und mehr junge Architekten machen sich selbstständig. Neben den großen staatlichen Designinstituten hat der Einfluss privater Architekturbüros bedeutend zugenommen. Diese Büros wurden in den Zeiten der Großbauprojekte gegründet, die Architekten mehr Chancen einräumten, Erfahrungen zu sammeln und ihre eigenen kreativen Ideen umzusetzen.

Architektonische Arbeiten kleinen Maßstabs und Arbeiten am Stadtrand
Bei den meisten vorgestellten Arbeiten handelt es sich um relativ kleine öffentliche Gebäude, die den Architekten beim Entwerfen und Gestalten sehr viele Freiheiten ließen. Öffentliche Gebäude unterliegen nicht den gleichen Auflagen und Einschränkungen wie der Wohnungsbau, der an strikte Vorschriften zu Belichtung, Funktion etc. gebunden ist. Während einige Projekte in urbanen Geschäftszentren liegen, befinden sich andere am Stadtrand oder in speziellen kulturellen oder universitären Bezirken. Gerade diese Projekte waren weniger den kommerziellen Interessen unterworfen, sondern boten mehr kreativen Freiraum.

Schlussfolgerung: Gibt es einen „chinesischen Weg" in der Architektur?
In den letzten drei Jahrzehnten hat China wirtschaftlich und gesellschaftlich enorme Fortschritte gemacht. Die Erfahrungen dieser Zeit zeigen, dass das Land einen „chinesischen Weg" nicht nur gehen kann, sondern muss. Das chinesische Experiment leistet heute einen eigenen Beitrag zur globalen Zivilisation, die so lange vom westlichen Vorbild bestimmt wurde. Wohin der „chinesische Weg" in der Wirtschaft führt, wird sich – gerade angesichts der globalen Wirtschaftskrise – zeigen. Aber im Bereich der Architektur müssen wir folgende Fragen beantworten: Ist die physische Gestalt moderner chinesischer Bauten und Städte ein qualitätvoller architektonischer Ausdruck des „chinesischen Modells"? Haben die architektonischen Experimente Chinas womöglich universale Folgen? Und schließlich: Wie viel kulturelle Zuversicht kann uns die zeitgenössische chinesische Architektur geben?

From Material to Space:
Aspects of a New Architecture in China

Eduard Kögel

Berlin-based critic, publisher, and curator in the field of architecture and urban development, editor of www.chinese-architects.com

The economic opening of the country in the 1980s brought with it an unstoppable construction boom that initially was handled primarily by government architectural practices. Before long they were joined by foreign architects with whose help the socialist construction industry sought to latch onto international trends. While most branches of industry were liberalized by the year 2000 and private actors admitted, due to the lack of clarity surrounding insurance issues in the field of architecture licenses were only awarded to private practices to a limited extent. In the mid-1990s, when foreign architects began to open their own offices in China, it also created opportunities for young Chinese colleagues. New hotel construction for an international public, residential buildings for an emerging middle class, cultural buildings for new leisure activities and private developers necessitated individual solutions, which the large state-run design institutes did not supply. Like the foreign practices that were only engaged for the design the young architects cooperated in the project execution with the large state licensed firms that were meanwhile run like private enterprises. A gray area soon emerged in which it was possible for small commissions from private clients outside the metropolises to be handled without the help of licensed firms. This led to the development of an independent scene producing work that also found praise outside China.

If we are to consider what concepts the first architects to operate independently pursued, then the question as to where they trained comes into play. Architects who studied in the early 1980s such as LIU Jiakun, TONG Ming and WANG Shu were not able to leave the country to extend their knowledge. Today, a stint abroad is almost inevitable for budding young architects. With this in mind it is a common practice to set up practices with partners from various countries, which are registered both in China and abroad. While locally trained architects sought to create solutions above all using the means available, returnees deployed conceptual and formal methods that were clearly influenced by international discourse.

The first two architects able to position themselves successfully in this context in the mid-1990s were **CHANG Yung Ho** with his firm Feichang Jianzhu in Beijing and LIU Jiakun in Chengdu. CHANG primarily tackled small annexes and conversion projects in the capital, but also others that remained unrealized or were closely related to art. His studies in the United States—he spent twelve years there as a student and lecturer—made it easier for him to communicate with international experts. As early as 1993 and thanks to his registration as an American architect, he was able to open the practice in Beijing with his wife LU Lijia. In subsequent years, he pursued new avenues in training with material experiments and founding a post-graduate course for architects at Beijing University.

For **LIU Jiakun,** the situation was a different one. He had trained as an architect in the late 1970s in Chongqing, and turned to literature in the late 1980s. Having booked several successes as an author, from 1993 he devoted himself to architecture again. Artist friends commissioned him to design studio houses in the rural environs of the metropolis of Chengdu in the Province Sichuan. What makes the small series of buildings so special is the vibrant force of the local materials and the simple composition of a few elements such as courtyard and wall. ZHAI Yongming, an author friend of his, wrote: "The rational portrayal on an architectural level can be identified in the theoretical framework of his narrations, but as regards the meaning of the architectural (doctrine) it combines everything that LIU hoped for: creating things under the control of reason that are no longer to be comprehended using reason."[1]

With LIU, the call for tradition does not remain abstract, but is also expressed in the important issue of structural realization: local workmen should be put in a position to actually realize the concepts in an appropriate quality. This is why details and components are tested with the construction firm responsible before being implemented in the building itself. LIU Jiakun stands out for his quest to maximize what is feasible, which he seeks to achieve by making the most of the inadequately trained workmen.

Thanks to **TONG Ming's** ingenious use of local materials in combination with contemporary usage concepts, his buildings reflect both historical phenomena and do justice to the modern resident's need for identity through a transformed Chinese design world. The sensitive treatment of proportions and scale serves to meld his buildings naturally with existing structures.

There is something more irritating about the work of **Amateur Architects,** WANG Shu and LU Wenyu, whose collage technique is not only based on traditional replicas but also on alienation. Given the size of the projects, the experimental approaches are not always implemented satisfactorily in construction terms. The recycling of used materials taken from torn-down buildings in the region is effectively a criticism of the old building culture being destroyed and in addition to introducing an historical patina also seeks to refer to the quality of the historical substance.

At **standardarchitecture**—established in 1999 in New York, returned in 2001 to Beijing—materials such as natural stone, brick or bamboo are carefully combined with urban references. This permits an influence of the exterior space, which is seen as a part of the building. Climatic conditions and extreme pressure regarding usages, which demand robust solutions are to be placed in balance with the aging quality of surfaces.

The practice **MADA s.p.a.m.** was also set up in New York by MA Qingyun, before he returned in 2000 to Shanghai. Ma saw the "negative aspects" in contemporary architectural developments in China as an opportunity and sought to gain as much liberty as possible from the speed in the construction process and the myriad of local restrictions.[2] By means of this strategy his urban renewal projects in Ningbo, Qingpu or Wuxi have contributed to urban space outside covered malls being regarded as desirable. Though the architectural quality of the property itself does not predominate, the overall compositions are characterized by staggering, superimposing and links with the surroundings, which creates a truly urban composition. What he creates are not just facilities for mass use, but lively quarters, which prove that even under today's conditions cities can be built as collective space using contemporary instruments. In smaller projects in the hinterlands, MA employed his conceptual approach to involve local workmen, who can submit their own ideas within a prescribed framework. Including workers in the creative process has a positive influence and increases both acceptance and maintenance by the later users.

As a partner of the practice urbanus—which was also established 1999 in the United States—ZHU Pei was one of the first returnees from abroad to set a new emphasis in his native country. In 2005, he and his partner TONG Wu founded **Studio Pei-Zhu.** The office's renown has spread beyond the country, given its zest in employing experimental materials, as in the case of Blur Hotel in Beijing, whose façade is composed of plastic elements, and its expressive designs for museums. It was only logical that Studio Pei-Zhu was one of the first practices to secure major projects outside China.

Atelier Z+ was established by ZHANG Bin and his partner ZHOU Wei in Shanghai in 2002. They particularly attracted attention with commissions for new buildings at Tongji University. The pressed glass panels used both for the interior and exterior of the building and Corten steel for the exterior skin, whereas timber combined with black steel was utilized for the interiors of the Sino-French-Center point to the search for haptic experiences in architecture. The sculptural design of the structure in combination with the material quality of the surface creates spatial qualities that are tailored to function and use.

Following her studies in Harvard and a time spent working for OMA in Rotterdam, XU Tiantian opened the firm **DnA_Design and Architecture** in 2004 in Beijing. With spectacular cultural and museum buildings, which nonetheless fit into their rural or urban context, XU succeeds in combining complex spatial programs with superimposing an organic linking of interior and exterior on structuralist approaches. This approach has, in less than five years, spawned several major buildings, which both reflect international developments but also point the way to an independent, contemporary, architecture culture.

Chinese architecture has undergone a remarkable development over the last fifteen years. Above all, as regards the materials used, the spatial compositions and urban insertion, gentle allusions transfer traditional elements into legible references, which attempt to find a contemporary expression for outdated topics. Those architects who rely on cheap manual labor for their buildings must know precisely what level of work they can expect. It is of little help to have studied abroad in these instances as such experiences must be made locally.

However, it can happen that such positive developments are hindered by further difficulties. After all, execution planning, building construction, and site supervision often lie in the hands of large licensed offices or the developers themselves neither of whom necessarily consult with the architectural designer. Add to this the lack of experience young firms have in dealing with a speedy decision and building process. Where there is too great a discrepancy between the aspired results and what the local construction industry can realistically achieve occasionally results in technical difficulties remaining unsolved. In this environment and given the present structure of the construction industry it is difficult to get technical innovations or new experimental inventions accepted. Another problem relates to how the use of a building is often only determined after its completion and without consulting the architects. Often specialized firms are selected in advance to do interior design work. They tend to hardly heed the architects' concepts and attempt instead to arrange the building's skin from the inside to suit the intended use. This can produce grotesque results in which the external shape only serves as a packaging to enclose the inner volumes. In order to establish a high-quality construction culture in the sense of the companies involved, the clients and the population, will require a lot of explanations, information, and experimentation to reconcile the needs of a mass culture with local options. However, a sustainable architectural culture that is characterized by materiality, space, and social prestige and is evidently the goal of a young generation of architects already indicates how contemporary architecture in China can also gain further relevance outside the country's borders.

1 Unpublished manuscript translated by Tanja Reith
2 Knutson, Peter: "Die Benefits des Schlechten." *Archplus* 168, (Feb. 2004): pp. 56f

Vom Material zum Raum:
Aspekte einer neuen Architektur in China

Eduard Kögel

Kritiker und Publizist aus Berlin, freier Kurator für Architektur und Städtebau, Redakteur von www.chinese-architects.com

Mit der ökonomischen Öffnung Chinas in den 1980er Jahren entwickelte sich ein ungebremster Bauboom, der zuerst vor allem von den staatlichen Architekturbüros bewältigt wurde. Schon bald kamen ausländische Architekten hinzu, mit deren Hilfe die sozialistische Bauwirtschaft versuchte, an internationale Trends anzuschließen. Während sich die meisten Wirtschaftszweige bis zur Jahrtausendwende liberalisierten und private Akteure zugelassen wurden, blieb bei den Architekten aufgrund ungeklärter Versicherungsfragen die Lizenzvergabe an private Büros sehr beschränkt. Mitte der 1990er Jahre, als die ausländischen Architekten selbst begannen, eigene Büros in China zu eröffnen, bekamen auch die jungen chinesischen Kollegen eine Chance. Hotelneubauten für ein internationales Publikum, Wohnbauten für die neue Mittelschicht, Kulturbauten für neue Bedürfnisse und private Bauherren forderten individuelle Lösungen, die von den großen staatlichen Designinstituten nicht geboten wurden. Wie die ausländischen Büros, die lediglich für den Entwurf beauftragt wurden, kooperierten die jungen Architekten für die Ausführung der Projekte mit den staatlich lizenzierten – und inzwischen privatwirtschaftlich organisierten – Großbüros. Bald schon entstand eine Grauzone, in der auch kleine Aufträge für private Bauherren außerhalb der Metropolen ohne die Hilfe der lizenzierten Büros realisiert werden konnten. Auf dieser Basis entwickelte sich eine eigenständige Szene, deren Werk auch im Ausland Anerkennung fand.

Stellt man die Frage nach den Konzepten der ersten unabhängig agierenden Architekten, so wird die Frage nach der Ausbildung bedeutsam. Die Anfang der 1980er Jahre studierenden Architekten, wie LIU Jiakun, TONG Ming und WANG Shu konnten das Land noch nicht für ihr Studium verlassen. Heute ist ein Auslandsaufenthalt für die erfolgreichen jungen Architekten fast unumgänglich. Aus diesen Erfahrungen entstehen oft Büros mit Partnern aus verschiedenen Ländern, die dann sowohl in China als auch im Ausland registriert sind. Während die lokal ausgebildeten Architekten vor allem mit den verfügbaren Möglichkeiten nach Lösungen suchten, war bei den Rückkehrern ein konzeptioneller und formaler Ansatz erkennbar, der deutlich vom internationalen Diskurs beeinflusst war.

Die beiden ersten Architekten, die sich in diesem Kontext Mitte der 1990er Jahre erfolgreich positionieren konnten, waren **CHANG Yung Ho** mit seinem Büro Feichang Jianzhu in Peking und LIU Jiakun in Chengdu. CHANG befasste sich vor allem mit kleinen Ein- und Umbauten in der Hauptstadt sowie mit Projekten, die unrealisiert geblieben sind oder im Grenzbereich zur Kunst angesiedelt waren. Sein Studium in den USA, wo er zwölf Jahre als Student und Lehrender verbrachte, erleichterte ihm die Kommunikation mit der internationalen Fachöffentlichkeit. Bereits 1993 konnte er zusammen mit seiner Frau LU Lijia, registriert als US-amerikanischer Architekt, das Büro in Peking eröffnen. Mit Materialexperimenten und der Gründung eines Aufbaustudiums für Architekten an der Pekinger Universität konnte er in den folgenden Jahren in der Ausbildung neue Wege beschreiten.

Für **LIU Jiakun** war die Situation eine andere. Er war als Architekt in den späten 1970er Jahren in Chongqing ausgebildet worden und wandte sich Ende der 1980er Jahre der Literatur zu. Nachdem er als Schriftsteller bereits einige Erfolge verbuchen konnte, befasste er sich ab 1993 wieder mit der Architektur. Befreundete Künstler beauftragten ihn mit der Planung von Studiohäusern im ländlichen Umfeld der Metropole Chengdu in der Provinz Sichuan. Die kleine Serie von Bauten lebt vor allem von der Kraft lokaler Materialien und der einfachen Komposition aus wenigen Elementen wie Hof und Mauer. Die befreundete Schriftstellerin ZHAI Yongming schrieb: „Die rationale Darstellung auf architektonischer Ebene lässt sich im theoretischen Rahmen seiner Erzählungen verorten, doch in Hinblick auf den Bedeutungsgehalt der Architektur(lehre) fasst sie wiederum alles zusammen, was sich LIU erhoffte: Unter der Kontrolle der Vernunft Dinge zu schaffen, die mit der Vernunft nicht mehr zu begreifen sind."[1]

Die Berufung auf die Tradition bleibt bei LIU nicht abstrakt, sondern drückt sich auch in der wichtigen Frage der bautechnischen Umsetzung aus: Die lokalen Handwerker sollen in die Lage versetzt werden, die Konzepte in ansprechender Qualität tatsächlich zu realisieren. Deshalb werden Details und Bauteile mit der ausführenden Firma erprobt, bevor sie am Bauwerk zur Ausführung kommen. Die besondere Qualität von LIU Jiakun liegt in der Suche nach dem Maximum des Machbaren, das er im Rahmen der Möglichkeiten der oft unzureichend ausgebildeten Handwerker sucht.

In **TONG Mings** Bauten sind durch die raffinierte Verwendung von lokalen Materialien in Kombination mit zeitgenössischen Nutzungskonzepten sowohl historische Erscheinungsbilder reflektiert wie auch dem heutigen Bedürfnis der Bewohner nach Identität durch eine transformierte chinesische Formenwelt Rechnung getragen. Der sensible Umgang mit Proportion und Maßstab fügt seine Bauten selbstverständlich in vorhandene Strukturen.

Etwas irritierender ist das Werk von **Amateur Architects** von WANG Shu und LU Wenyu, deren Collagetechnik sowohl von tradierten Abbildern ausgeht als auch von der Verfremdung. Durch die Größe der Projekte sind die experimentellen Ansätze nicht immer in bautechnisch befriedigender Weise gelöst. Die Wiederverwendung von gebrauchten Materialien, aus Abbruchhäusern in der Region, versteht sich als Kritik an der Vernichtung der alten Baukultur und will neben der Übernahme einer historischen Patina auch auf die Qualität des historischen Bestandes verweisen.

Bei **standardarchitecture** – 1999 in New York gegründet und 2001 nach Peking zurückgekehrt – wird sorgfältige Materialverwendung wie zum Beispiel von Naturstein, Backstein oder Bambus mit urbanen Beziehungen kombiniert. Damit lässt sich der Außenraum prägen, der als Bestandteil des Bauwerks gesehen wird. Die klimatischen Bedingungen und der extreme Nutzungsdruck, die nach robusten Lösungen verlangen, sind mit der Alterungsfähigkeit der Oberflächen in Balance gesetzt.

Das Büro **MADA s.p.a.m.** wurde von MA Qingyun ebenfalls in New York gegründet, bevor er 2000 nach Shanghai zurückkehrte.

MA hat das „Schlechte" in der heutigen Architekturentwicklung in China als Chance begriffen und versucht aus der Geschwindigkeit im Bauprozess und aus den vielen Beschränkungen vor Ort eine möglichst große Freiheit zu gewinnen.[2] Mit dieser Strategie haben seine Stadtsanierungsprojekte in Ningbo, Qingpu oder Wuxi dazu beigetragen, dass heute auch der urbane Raum außerhalb geschlossener Malls als erstrebenswert angesehen wird. Zwar dominiert dabei nicht die architektonische Qualität des Objekts, aber die gesamten Kompositionen sind geprägt von Schichtungen, Überlagerungen und Verknüpfungen mit dem Umfeld, die eine wirklich urbane Struktur entstehen lassen. Zusammen mit dem Nutzungsdruck durch die Masse entstanden lebendige Quartiere, die beweisen, dass auch unter heutigen Bedingungen Stadt als kollektiver Raum mit zeitgenössischen Mitteln gebaut werden kann. Bei kleineren Projekten im Hinterland hat MA mit seiner konzeptionellen Art die lokalen Handwerker eingebunden, die ihre Vorstellungen in einem vorgegebenen Rahmen einbringen können. Die Einbindung der Arbeiter in den kreativen Prozess hat positive Wirkung und erleichtert die Akzeptanz sowie die Pflege durch die späteren Nutzer.

ZHU Pei gehörte als Partner des Büros urbanus – das sich ebenfalls 1999 in den USA gründete – zu den ersten, die aus dem Ausland in der Heimat neue Impulse setzten. 2005 gründete er zusammen mit seiner Partnerin TONG Wu das **Studio Pei-Zhu**. Mit experimentellen Materialien wie beim Blur Hotel in Peking, dessen Fassade aus Kunststoffelementen zusammengesetzt ist, und mit expressiven Formen für Museen ist das Büro nicht nur national erfolgreich. Als eines der ersten Büros konnte Studio Pei-Zhu auch wichtige Projekte im Ausland für sich gewinnen.

Atelier Z+ wurde von ZHANG Bin und seiner Partnerin ZHOU Wei 2002 in Shanghai gegründet. Sie konnten vor allem mit den Aufträgen für neue Gebäude an der Tongji-Universität auf sich aufmerksam machen. Die gepressten Glaspaneele im Innen- wie im Außenbereich des Architekturgebäudes sowie Cortenstahl als Material für die Außenhaut und Holz in Kombination mit schwarzem Stahl für die Innenräume des Sino-French-Center verweisen auf die Suche nach haptischen Erfahrungen in der Architektur. Die plastische Gestaltung der Baukörper in Verbindung mit der Materialität der Oberfläche schafft räumliche Qualitäten, die auf die Funktion und Nutzung abgestimmt sind.

XU Tiantian hat 2004 nach ihrem Studium in Harvard und einer Mitarbeit bei OMA in Rotterdam ihr Büro **DnA_Design and Architecture** in Peking gegründet. Mit spektakulären Kultur- und Museumsbauten, die sich dennoch in ihren landschaftlichen oder urbanen Kontext fügen, gelingt es XU, komplexe Raumprogramme mit einer Überlagerung von strukturalistischen Ansätzen mit einer organischen Verknüpfung von Außenraum und Innenraum zu verbinden. In weniger als fünf Jahren entstanden so mehrere große Bauten, die sowohl die internationalen Entwicklungen reflektieren als auch den Weg in eine eigenständige zeitgenössische Baukultur weisen.

In der chinesischen Architektur hat sich in den letzten 15 Jahren Bemerkenswertes entwickelt. Vor allem im Hinblick auf Materialverwendung, Raumkomposition und städtebauliche Einbindung werden mit zarten Andeutungen traditionelle Elemente in lesbare Hinweise übertragen, die versuchen, überkommene Themen in einer zeitgenössischen Form zum Ausdruck zu bringen. Die Architekten, die sich mit ihren Bauten auf die billige Arbeitskraft und damit auf eine handwerkliche Ausführung einlassen, müssen den Stand der Ausführungsqualität genau kennen. Dazu hilft das Studium im Ausland nur bedingt, denn die Erfahrungen müssen vor Ort gemacht werden.

Die hier dargestellte positive Entwicklung wird jedoch in mancherlei Hinsicht durch weitere Schwierigkeiten behindert. Denn Ausführungsplanung ebenso wie Baukonstruktion und Bauüberwachung liegen oft ohne Rückkopplung an die Entwurfsverfasser in den Händen lizenzierter Großbüros oder bei den Bauherren selbst. Dazu kommt die fehlende Erfahrung der jungen Büros bei einem rasanten Entscheidungs- und Bauprozess, der bei zu großer Differenz zwischen angestrebter Ausführung und realen Möglichkeiten der lokalen Bauwirtschaft manches Mal aufgrund ungelöster technischer Schwierigkeiten abgebrochen werden muss. Konstruktive Innovationen oder experimentelle Neuerfindungen sind in der jetzigen Struktur des Bauwesens deshalb nur schwer durchsetzbar. Ein weiteres Problem ist die Art der Nutzung, die oft erst nach Fertigstellung der Bauten – und ohne Rücksprache mit den Architekten – festgelegt wird. Oft ist der Innenausbau von vorneherein auf spezialisierte Firmen verlagert. Diese scheren sich wenig um die Konzepte der Architekten, sondern versuchen, die Gebäudehülle von innen her für die am Ende vorgesehene Nutzung einzurichten. Dabei entstehen groteske Maskeraden, bei denen die äußere Form nur als Verpackung das Volumen umspannt. Für die Etablierung einer qualitätvollen Baukultur im Bewusstsein der beteiligten Firmen, der Bauherren, aber auch der Bevölkerung braucht es deshalb noch viel Aufklärung und Experimente, um die Bedürfnisse einer Massenkultur mit den Möglichkeiten vor Ort zu vereinbaren. Eine nachhaltige architektonische Kultur, die von Materialität, Raum und gesellschaftlicher Bedeutung geprägt ist und die ganz offensichtlich von einer jungen Generation von Architekten angestrebt wird, zeigt jedoch bereits heute den Weg, auf dem die zeitgenössische Architektur in China in Zukunft auch außerhalb des Landes weiter an Relevanz gewinnen kann.

1 Unveröffentlichtes Manuskript, übersetzt von Tanja Reith
2 Knutson, Peter: „Die Benefits des Schlechten". In: *Archplus* 168, Feb. 2004: S. 56f.

Defining a Contemporary Chinese Architecture:
The Fusion of *Tao* and *Fa*

Robert Ivy

FAIA, Editor in Chief of *Architectural Record*, Vice President and Editorial Director of McGraw-Hill Construction Publications, New York

China's architectural evolution has occurred with blinding speed. In June 1999, an international gathering of 4,000 architects and planners, together with 2,000 students, visited the 20th UIA (International Union of Architects) Congress. While the ostensible theme of the symposium concerned the development of cities worldwide in the twenty-first century, the focus of participants lay in exploring a new country.

Professor WU Liangyong of Tsinghua University introduced principles for global urban development in a document entitled, "The Beijing Charter." Drawing from his knowledge of Chinese history, in particular the development of city form, he described the framework that had guided China's building traditions: "Classical Chinese philosophers went to great pains to pinpoint the differences between methodology (alternatively translated as *Dao* or *Tao*), which concerns an intellectual framework, and methods *(Fa)* which deal with specific techniques." He challenged those present to consider principles to guide future growth, such as the "fusion of architecture, landscape architecture, and city planning," and to capture the benefits of the ongoing technological revolution while remembering the benefits of "indigenous culture."

Professor WU's words seem prescient. If, ten years ago, examples reflecting the highest standards of modernity in design and construction were limited to specific, showcase buildings in China, building materials and systems were advancing, however, to meet the demands of demographic and economic shifts. At the same time, intellectual discussions and debates were resulting in a framework that would result in change. The *Tao* and *Fa* were accelerating toward a kind of genetic fusion as the global economy quickly grew.

The eight architects and their work represented herein represent the realization of the ideals Prof. WU outlined. They combine many of the basic principles, as well as the means and materials available to contemporary Chinese architects; and they apply not only to individual structures, but sometimes to entire precincts and cities. Moreover, they attempt to fuse the spirit of modernism with the specifics of place and people, combining topography, climate, and geography (among other characteristics) with utility and human need. In a sense, they are grappling with, and realizing some success, in defining a contemporary Chinese architecture.

They follow in the wake of a generation of global architects who, for over a decade, have sought and found major commissions in China. Among the first American architects to engage with Chinese clients were the architects John Portman, whose Ritz Carlton Hotel on Nanjing Xi Lu in Shanghai Center (1990) still serves as a kind of urban center, and I. M. Pei, who designed the Frangrant Hills Hotel near Beijing (1982), and subsequently designed, with his sons, the massive, yet light-filled, Bank of China in Beijing (2000). Chinese clients sought leading practitioners from around the world for their most important projects, commissioning the French architect Paul Andreu to design the Shanghai Pudong Airport (1999) and, most visibly, the ovoid National Grand Theater in Beijing (2008).

Size and height, together with the prestige of the designer, have combined to produce work that literally rises above the ordinary. For the Jin Mao Tower, a mixed-use project in Pudong, Shanghai, the architects Skidmore, Owings and Merrill, working with a local design institute, conceived, at eighty-eight stories, the tallest building in China, that can compete with the Oriental Pearl Tower, Shanghai's other iconic tower on the Pudong skyline.

The approach of the Olympic games in 2008 brought a kind of superlative list of accomplishments with the increased design and construction, particularly to the Beijing skyline. Projects vied for singularity, whether newest, largest, or most distinctive. For CCTV, the architect Rem Koolhaas with partner Ole Scheeren and his firm OMA, together with the engineering firm Arup, created a massive complex linking two towers (with 44 and 54 stories respectively) above the Beijing streets (2002–2010). Projects at the Olympics themselves provided an opportunity to showcase prowess, when combined with the skills of international designers such as Herzog & de Meuron, and Arup at the Beijing National Stadium (2008), the bird's nest. Designed by a consortium including the architectural firm Foster and Partners, again with Arup, Terminal 3 at Beijing Capital Airport (2004) was the largest terminal in the world for several years, a title since surrendered to Dubai. All of these projects gained significant media attention.

While the internationally fueled, highly prominent projects were occurring, however, other forces were at play in China that have resulted in positive results for contemporary architecture. Schools of architecture, such as Beijing's Tsinghua University and Shanghai's Tongji University, encouraged dialogue and exchange of lecturer as well as student. Universities have been active in discussing contemporary issues such as the role of historic preservation in a rapidly developing country, with research and conservation realized by practitioner/academics such as Prof. CHANG Qing at Tongji University. Additionally, Chinese architects like CHANG Yung Ho and MA Qing Yung now serve as deans at schools of architecture abroad, at MIT and the University of Southern California, respectively.

The major design institutes, and in particular their design studios led by significant practitioners such as Cui Kai at the China Design Institute, are developing indigenous talent, many of whom have collaborated with international designers. Architectural publications grew in sophistication and scope within China, bringing to light the best of contemporary Chinese and worldwide architectural work, such as Beijing-based *World Architecture* and *Time + Architecture* from Shanghai.

The development of collateral disciplines, including engineering and landscape architecture, has enriched the architectural dialogue. Turenscape, a landscape design studio led by Dean YU Kongjian, in conjunction with Peking University, has engaged former urban industrial sites, among other projects, reinvesting them with new open spaces. A new generation of planners and government officials, like Dr. SUN Jiwei, formerly in Qingpu and now District Mayor of Jiading (a satellite city of Shanghai), has been working at re-envisioning cities in a country in which a tide of rural village dwellers will eventually move from farm to city.

Simultaneously, an explosion of the arts has fueled the architectural dialogue. The loosening of restrictions of expression coupled with rising economies and widespread interest in Chinese expression within and outside of China has resulted in a flourishing of the arts. Visual artists like Ai Weiwei, who has designed constructed installations and entire buildings, blur the line between art and architecture, encouraging other architects to reciprocate.

Commerce has abetted the prosperity of the arts, and, in the process, has fueled architectural work. At one level, galleries sought cheap, simple housing in converted industrial facilities—prized for their large, open spaces and light—which has resulted in the transformation of the successful Factory 798 or Dashanzi Arts District in Beijing, or Shanghai's M50. Individual spaces offer architects and interior designers pre-existing structures, replete with their own texture and histories, on which artists and designers can overlay their contemporary work.

What constitutes contemporary architecture in China? Apart from the massive design institutes, which sometimes number over 1,000 people, these eight architects have established individual, design-centric practices that explore the notion. Difficult to characterize as a group without running the risk of oversimplification, they deal nevertheless with certain common themes, including the question of authenticity in a multipartite, multivalent world. Varying in the scale of projects that they engage with, from the individual house to entire city plans, and actual size of practice, as well as their proclivities to work outside China—they all are characterized by going far beyond what the West would categorize as the momentary fashion in search of an architecture more fully suited to the unique cultures and settings of China.

The work of all eight architects included here could be described as using bold, geometric forms for new construction, though none of the geometries herein reflect the recent Western tendencies toward biomorphic form-making—a tendency encouraged by computer technology. At the same time, when they engage with existing structures, such as in historic urban neighborhoods, or at a smaller scale, they acknowledge the differences and their work becomes finer in scale and texture. An evident engagement with landscape characterizes many of the projects shown, in which hillsides flow around or even into the human-built structures, and roofs sometimes serve as additional habitable planes.

Their concern for sustainability, so overtly described in the rest of the world, resides in more traditional building technologies and strategies, such as solar orientation, building mass, screening, and natural ventilation, rather than the active, elaborate systems that are typical of European or American design. In a country with a long history of urbanism, the social utility of projects, including their public spaces, seems evident. And architects in China must be constantly aware of variables of construction, where refinement of detail must sometimes give way to overall effect, depending on the abilities and budgets of their clientele.

Building materials (the *Fa* of Professor WU's discourse) help to define the appropriate architecture for time and place, none with greater force or combined distinction than stone. Architects like Liu Jiakun extensively employ the use of stone, nowhere to greater effect than in his Luyeyuan Stone Sculpture Museum. There, small, incremental pieces of native stone have been stacked into walls and columns to house early Buddhist works of art, their silvery gray coloration in subtle contradistinction to the white walls, glazing, and metal railing that define the interiors. Form and texture are highlighted by high clerestory windows, which throw individual elements, whether artwork or stone, into fine-grained relief.

Other architects using stone for its natural tendencies to produce mass and apparent solidity include standardarchitecture. At the Namchabaw Visitor Center, the elements have been reduced to a bare minimum, in which irregular stone pieces are laid in massive walls, creating strong box-like forms surmounted by a simple concrete roof, painted white. The distinction of elements, and the reduction in number and kind, add to the overall powerful effect, which must coexist with the mountainous topography and announce its human making and intention.

At his father's house, set high above the Jade Village in the ancient area near X'ian, MA Qingyun placed smooth river stones, stacked vertically, in a wall. The cumulative summary of this iterative process serves to create a tactile, sensory response: it creates the desire to touch. Collected into a walled courtyard, the stone wall abstracts nature while making it actual and present, merging the elements of nature with human interaction and art.

Brick and glazed tile go beyond the found object to the articles of industry and manufacture. The spectacular surfaces of the Ceramic House by WANG Shu combine a glazed tile in a random pattern that varies in coloration from tobacco brown to celadon to light blue. Placed on both walls and floors, particularly on a sloping wall that follows a hill's contours into and onto the floor of the building, the tiles flow like water and alter the austerity of the geometric forms with an apparent plasticity. Material trumps reality.

Materials deployed into systems can be used in combination to create screening effects. The architect TONG Ming, addressing a narrow urban redevelopment at Suquan Yuan, was faced with how to create identity for a development project that lacked tenants. His solution for the concrete teahouse that provides the entrance to the property is screened, with wooden screens in elaborate geometric patterns reminiscent of older motifs, backing long glazed openings that admit light to a long interior corridor.

For the Sino-French Center at Tongji University in Shanghai, the architect ZHANG Bin deploys material for its own effect, allowing large expanses of steel (Corten-type, pre-rusted steel panels) to create texture, while interiors are characterized by planes of wood that contrast with the exterior, bringing warmth to the more austere exterior.

ZHU Pei, like other Chinese architects, has worked at several scales, with a variety of architectural issues. The disappearance of the *hutong*, a critical question for modern China, finds a contemporary resolution in ZHU Pei's Cai Guoqiang Courtyard house. There, the original building fabric has been restored where appropriate, while the architect has inserted a new studio with a glazed wall into the design. Additionally, interiors feature wood walls with continuous surfaces enriched by wood screens in a gridded pattern that are in dialogue with traditional Chinese ornament and usage. Like his peers, he has engaged the larger scale, most notably at Digital Beijing, where giant slab-like forms hint at the power and impenetrability of the computer.

At the scale of the neighborhood, XU Tiantian has expanded the residential alternatives for artists in Beijing at the Songzhuang Artist Residence. When the arts movement threatened to overwhelm the 798 district, many artists chose to move. XU Tiantian has designed twenty individual housing units facing a fishpond, where artists can live and work. The overall neighborhood achieves an urban quality that underscores the personal work of the inhabitants, while allowing for their communal interests and work.

From the house to the precinct to the city, a generation is taking Chinese architecture in new directions. Working independently, working collaboratively, enriching their own intellectual discourse from multiple sources, and under intense interest from the rest of the world, in a country where designing for growth and change have critical importance, they represent the vanguard of a people seeking new self-definitions while transforming themselves for a new century, achieving a "fusion of architecture, landscape architecture, and city planning."

Definition einer zeitgenössischen chinesischen Architektur:
Die Verbindung von *Tao* und *Fa*

Robert Ivy

FAIA, Chefredakteur von *Architectural Record*, Vizepräsident und Editorial Director von McGraw-Hill Construction Publications, New York

Die Architektur in China entwickelt sich mit rasender Geschwindigkeit. Im Juni 1999 kamen 4000 internationale Architekten und 2000 Studenten zum 20. Kongress der UIA (Union Internationale des Architectes) nach Peking. Offiziell war das Symposium der weltweiten Stadtentwicklung des 21. Jahrhunderts gewidmet, aber die Aufmerksamkeit der Teilnehmer richtete sich viel mehr auf das neu zu entdeckende Land China.
Unter dem Titel „Charta von Peking" stellte Professor WU Liangyong von der Tsinghua Universität Richtlinien für die globale Stadtentwicklung vor. Vor dem Hintergrund der chinesischen Geschichte, besonders der Stadtentwicklung, beschrieb er die Rahmenbedingungen, unter denen sich Chinas Bautraditionen herausgebildet hatten: „Klassische chinesische Philosophen legten großen Wert darauf, die Unterschiede zwischen Methodologie (*Dao* bzw. *Tao* genannt) als intellektuellem Rahmen und den Methoden (*Fa*), die mit bestimmten Techniken zu tun haben, genau zu definieren." Er forderte die Anwesenden auf, die Grundlagen zukünftigen Wachstums zu überdenken – beispielsweise die „Fusion von Architektur, Landschaftsarchitektur und Stadtplanung" –, die Vorteile der gegenwärtigen technologischen Revolution zu nutzen, dabei aber gleichzeitig das Wohl der „einheimischen Kultur" im Auge zu behalten.
Professor WUs Worte scheinen prophetisch. Vor gerade einmal zehn Jahren beschränkte sich anspruchsvolle moderne Architektur in China noch auf einige wenige Vorzeigegebäude. Seitdem wurden die Baumaterialien und -techniken jedoch – mit Blick auf die demografischen und ökonomischen Veränderungen – stetig weiterentwickelt. Intellektuelle Diskussionen und Debatten trugen das ihre zu einer Veränderung bei. Während die Weltwirtschaft wuchs und wuchs, steuerten *Tao* und *Fa* gewissermaßen auf eine genetische Verschmelzung zu.
Die acht hier vorgestellten Architekten und ihre Arbeiten repräsentieren die Umsetzung der von Professor WU beschriebenen Ideale und Grundprinzipien. Ihre Arbeiten zeigen die Bandbreite an Möglichkeiten und Materialien, die zeitgenössischen Architekten zur Verfügung stehen – vom einzelnen Gebäude bis zur Planung ganzer Stadtviertel und Städte. Allen ist gemein, dass sie zwischen Moderne und lokalen Architekturtraditionen vermitteln wollen und dabei (unter anderem) die spezifischen Gegebenheiten von Topografie, Klima und Geografie mit Funktionalität und individuellen Anforderungen zu vereinen suchen. Sie suchen gewissermaßen nach einer Definition zeitgenössischer chinesischer Architektur – mit einigem Erfolg.
Damit treten sie in die Fußstapfen einer Generation von global tätigen Architekten, die in China seit über einem Jahrzehnt große Aufträge umgesetzt haben. Unter den ersten amerikanischen Architekten, die mit chinesischen Bauherren zusammenarbeiteten, befanden sich John Portman, dessen Ritz Carlton Hotel (1990) auf der Nanjing Xi Lu im Zentrum Shanghais noch heute als eine Art Stadtzentrum dient, und I.M. Pei, der 1982 das Xiangshan (Fragrant Hill) Hotel bei Peking und 2000 mit seinen Söhnen die massive, doch lichtdurchflutete Bank of China in Peking entwarf.

Für ihre wichtigsten Gebäude suchten sich chinesische Kunden renommierte internaionale Architekten. Unter anderem engagierten sie den französischen Architekten Paul Andreu für den Flughafen Shanghai Pudong (1999) und – als bekanntestes Beispiel – das eiförmige Große Chinesische Nationaltheater in Peking (2008).
Ihre Größe und ihr Umfang und das Prestige der Architekten heben diese Projekte buchstäblich aus der Masse heraus. Mit dem 88-stöckigen Jin Mao Tower in Shanghai-Pudong haben Skidmore, Owings & Merrill, in Zusammenarbeit mit einem örtlichen Designinstitut, den höchsten Turm Chinas erbaut, der es mit dem Oriental Pearl Tower, Shanghais anderer Ikone in der Skyline von Pudong, aufnehmen kann. Die Olympischen Spiele 2008 bescherten insbesondere der Pekinger Skyline eine Flut von Neubauten, die alle um den Titel des größten oder markantesten Gebäudes wetteiferten. Für CCTV schuf Rem Koolhaas mit Ole Scheeren und seinem Büro OMA in Zusammenarbeit mit der Ingenieursfirma Arup von 2002 bis 2010 ein massives, auskragendes Gebäude, das zwei Türme (mit 44 bzw. 54 Stockwerken) über den Straßen von Peking vereinigt. In der Zusammenarbeit mit internationalen Spitzenarchitekten ließ sich auch die eigene Leistungsfähigkeit eindrucksvoll unter Beweis stellen, wie etwa beim Nationalstadion, dem Vogelnest, in Peking (2008) von Herzog & de Meuron und Arup. Der Terminal 3 des Beijing Capital Airport – entworfen von Foster and Partners und Arup – war für einige Jahre das größte Flughafengebäude der Welt, bis es diesen Titel an Dubai abtreten musste.
Parallel zu diesen international befeuerten, höchst prestigeträchtigen Bauten wurden in China allerdings auch andere Projekte geschmiedet, die die zeitgenössische Architektur positiv beeinflussten. Architekturschulen wie die Tsinghua Universität in Peking und die Tongji Universität in Shanghai regten den Dialog und Austausch von Studenten und Lehrenden an. Die Universitäten beteiligten sich aktiv an der Diskussion gegenwärtiger Probleme, etwa dem Schutz historischer Substanz, wobei sich lehrende, praktizierende Architekten wie Professor CHANG Qing von der Tongji Universität der Erforschung und Erhaltung der Gebäude widmeten. Außerdem leiten einige chinesische Architekten wie CHANG Yung Ho und MA Chingyun namhafte ausländische Architekturhochschulen (MIT bzw. University of Southern California). Die großen Designinstitute und besonders ihre Entwurfsabteilungen, die von bekannten Vertretern wie CUI Kai am China Design Institute geführt werden, bringen einheimische Talente hervor, die vielfach mit internationalen Entwerfern zusammengearbeitet haben. Die Architekturzeitschriften in China – *World Architecture* aus Peking und *Time + Architecture* aus Shanghai – haben an Qualität und Vielfalt zugelegt und die besten nationalen und internationalen Architekturprojekte veröffentlicht.
Auch das Ingenieurwesen und die Landschaftsarchitektur machten einen Entwicklungssprung und ein reger architektonischer Dialog ist entstanden. Turenscape, ein Landschaftsarchitekturbüro unter der Leitung von Dekan YU Kongjian, das eng mit der Beijing University zusammenarbeitet, hat sich unter anderem mit der Konversion ehemaliger Industrieflächen zu städtischen Freiräumen hervorgetan. Eine neue Generation von Planern und Beamten wie Dr. SUN Ji Wie (ehemals in Qingpu und nun Kreisbürgermeister von Jiading, einer Vorstadt von Shanghai) arbeitet an der Neukonzeptionierung von Städten, um die Flut der Arbeitsmigranten aus den ländlichen Gebieten aufzufangen.
Nahrung erhielt der architektonische Dialog außerdem durch eine Explosion der Künste, beflügelt durch die Lockerung von Zensurbestimmungen genauso wie durch das Wirtschaftswachstum und das wachsende Interesse an chinesischer Kunst im In- und Ausland. Darstellende Künstler wie Ai Weiwei, der bauliche Installationen und auch Gebäude entworfen hat, verwischen die Grenze zwischen Kunst und Architektur und ermutigen andere Architekten, sich ihrerseits zu äußern.
Der wirtschaftliche Markt hat den Aufschwung der Kunst begünstigt und zugleich die Architektur beflügelt. Zahlreiche Galerien suchten sich günstige, einfache Räume in umgebauten Industrie-

anlagen, die wegen ihrer großzügigen, freien und lichten Räumlichkeiten sehr beliebt sind. Erfolgreiche Umbauten sind zum Beispiel die Factory 798, der Dashanzi Kunstbezirk in Peking oder M50 in Shanghai. Viele dieser Räume sind buchstäblich vollgepropft mit Texturen, mit Geschichte … eine Fundgrube für Architekten und Innenarchitekten und eine Folie, die Künstler und Gestalter mit ihren eigenen Arbeiten überlagern können.

Was macht nun aber die zeitgenössische chinesische Architektur aus? Fernab der riesigen Designinstitute mit oft mehr als 1000 Mitarbeitern haben die hier vorgestellten acht Architekten kleine, entwurfsorientierte Büros geschaffen, die ihre Disziplin immer wieder neu hinterfragen. Als Gruppe sind sie nur schwer miteinander zu vergleichen und doch beschäftigen sie sich mit gemeinsamen Themen, wie der Frage nach Authentizität in einer vielgestaltigen und vielfältigen Welt. Obwohl sie sich in der Bedeutung der Projekte (vom einzelnen Haus bis zu ganzen Stadtentwürfen), der Größe der Büros und ihrem Engagement (zum Teil arbeiten sie international) unterscheiden, ist ihnen allen gemein, dass sie – anstatt den im Westen jeweils ausgerufenen Trends zu folgen – nach einer seriösen Architektursprache suchen, die den lokalen kulturellen Zusammenhängen und Orten Chinas stärker gerecht wird.

An den Neubauprojekten aller acht Büros fallen die ausdrucksstarken geometrischer Formen ins Auge, doch keine dieser Geometrien spiegelt die jüngste, von der Computertechnologie ausgelöste westliche Mode biomorpher Formgebung wider. Gleichzeitig wissen sie beim Umgang mit dem Bestand – bei historischen Stadtvierteln genauso wie bei kleineren Projekten – zu differenzieren und den Blick für die Feinheiten in Maßstab und Textur zu schärfen. Viele Projekte nehmen deutlichen Bezug auf die umgebende Landschaft oder beziehen sie direkt in die Bauten ein, Dächer dienen manchmal als zusätzliche Nutzfläche.

Ihr Beitrag zur weltweit so intensiv geführten Nachhaltigkeitsdebatte liegt eher in traditionellen Bauweisen und -konzepten – Berücksichtigung von Sonnenausrichtung, Gebäudemasse, Schichten und natürlicher Lüftung – als in den aktiven, aufwändigen Systemen, die westliche Projekte auszeichnen. Die Frage nach dem gesellschaftlichen Nutzen von Bauprojekten und öffentlichem Raum scheint in einem Land mit langer städtebaulicher Geschichte auf der Hand zu liegen. Außerdem müssen Architekten in China immer die besonderen Baubedingungen im Blick haben, wobei die Ausgestaltung im Detail manchmal dem Gesamteindruck den Vortritt lassen muss – je nach Fähigkeit und Budget der Bauherren.

Baumaterialien (das *Fa* in Professor WUs Rede) helfen bei der Definition einer der Zeit und dem Ort angemessenen Architektur, dabei besitzt kein Material größere Kraft oder Komplexität als Stein. So setzen Architekten wie LIU Jiakun Stein vielfach ein, die beeindruckendste Wirkung entfaltet er vielleicht im Luyeyuan Stone Sculpture Museum. Steine aus der Region wurden zu Wänden und Stützen geschichtet und bilden Räume für frühe buddhistische Kunstwerke. Ihre silbergraue Farbe steht im subtilen Kontrast zu den weißen Wänden, der Verglasung und den Metallhandläufen, die die Innenräume bestimmen. Form und Textur werden von hohen Lichtschlitzen betont, welche einzelnen Elementen wie beispielsweise den Kunstexponaten oder dem Stein ein feines Relief verleihen.

Zu den Architekten, die Stein aufgrund seiner natürlichen massiven Eigenschaften und offenkundigen Stabilität einsetzen, gehört auch das Büro standardarchitecture. Beim Numchabawa Besucherzentrum sind die Elemente auf ein Minimum reduziert und unregelmäßige Natursteine in massive Wände eingelassen worden. Dabei entstanden quaderförmige Formen mit einem einfachen, weiß gestrichenen Betondach darüber. Die Differenzierung der Elemente und deren Reduzierung in Art und Anzahl tragen zu einem starken Gesamteindruck bei, der sich in die Berglandschaft einfügt und doch seine Gemachtheit und seinen Zweck erkennen lassen.

Im Haus seines Vaters, das hoch über dem Jade Village im historischen Bezirk nahe Xi'an liegt, hat MA Chingyun abgeschliffene Flusssteine zu Wänden aufgeschichtet. Das Gesamtergebnis dieses iterativen Prozesses bewirkt eine sinnliche Reaktion: Man möchte das Gebäude berühren. Die Steinwände, die einen ummauerten Hof bilden, sind gleichzeitig abstrakte wie authentische und präsente Natur und verbinden natürliche Elemente mit menschlichem Wirken und Kunst.

Ziegel und glasierte Fliesen sind nicht mehr vorgefundenes, natürliches Material, sondern Produkte von Industrie und Handwerk. Die spektakulären Oberflächen des Ceramic House von WANG Shu bestehen aus glasierten Fliesen in losem Raster, in Farben von Tabakbraun zu Seladongrün bis Hellblau. Sie sind auf Wänden wie Böden angeordnet – besonders auf den geneigten Wänden und der Rampe, die dem Gelände folgen –, fließen wie Wasser und brechen somit die Strenge der geometrischen Formen mit fassbarer Plastizität auf: Material überflügelt hier die Realität.

In Systemen angewandte Materialien können in Kombination verwendet werden, um eine transparente Schichtung zu erreichen. TONG Ming stand bei der Bearbeitung des engen Grundstücks beim urbanen Sanierungsprojekt Suquanyuan vor der Frage, wie man einem Entwicklungsvorhaben, dem die Mieter fehlten, eine eigene Identität geben könne. Seine Lösung für den Stahlbetonbau des Teehauses, das den Eingang zum Areal bildet, waren schirmartige Schichten, Holzpaneele mit kunstvollen geometrischen Mustern, die traditionellen Motiven gleichen, vor hohen Fensteröffnungen stehen und den langen Innengang beleuchten.

Für das Sino French Center der Tongji Universität Shanghai verwendete der Architekt ZHANG Bin Materialien um ihrer Eigenschaften willen und erzeugte mit großen Flächen aus Corten-Stahl eine Textur, während er das Innere im Kontrast zur Fassade aus Holzflächen entwickelte und dadurch einen warmen Kontrapunkt zur strengeren Fassade erreichte.

Wie andere chinesische Architekten hat auch ZHU Pei verschiedene Maßstäbe und architektonische Themen bearbeitet. Sein Hofhaus für CAI Guoqiang reagiert auf zeitgenössische Weise auf eine der kritischen Fragen der Stadtplanung im heutigen China, auf das Verschwinden der Hutongs. Hier wurde die Originalsubstanz des Gebäudes dort, wo es angemessen war, restauriert und ein neues Atelier mit einer verglasten Fassade in den Entwurf integriert. Die Innenräume werden von Holzwänden mit durchgängigen Oberflächen bestimmt und durch hölzerne, ornamentierte Gitter bereichert, die sich auf die Tradition beziehen. Wie seine Mitstreiter hat auch er im größeren Maßstab gearbeitet, besonders für das Projekt Digital Beijing, bei dem riesige, scheibenartige Formen die Macht und Undurchdringlichkeit des Computers andeuten.

Im Maßstab eines Stadtviertels hat XU Tiantian die Songzhuang Artist Residence um weitere Wohnungen für Pekinger Künstler erweitert. Als die Kunstszene den District 798 zu erdrücken drohte, entschlossen sich viele Künstler zum Umzug. XU Tiantian hat 20 individuelle, zu einem Fischteich hin orientierte Wohneinheiten entworfen, in denen Künstler wohnen und arbeiten können. Das gesamte Viertel erreicht eine städtische Qualität, die die persönliche Arbeit der Bewohner unterstreicht und ihren gemeinschaftlichen Interessen und Tätigkeiten Raum lässt.

Vom Haus zum Stadtbezirk zur Stadt lenkt eine Generation von Architekten die chinesische Architektur in eine neue Richtung. Sie arbeiten unabhängig oder gemeinschaftlich, speisen ihren eigenen intellektuellen Diskurs aus verschiedenen Quellen, genießen große Aufmerksamkeit in aller Welt und arbeiten dabei in einem Land, in welchem der Planung von Wachstum und Veränderung kritische Bedeutung zukommt: Sie sind die Avantgarde eines Volkes, das nach einer neuen Selbstbestimmung sucht und sich dabei für ein neues Jahrhundert rüstet. Diese Architekten erreichen eine „Fusion von Architektur, Landschaftsarchitektur und Stadtplanung."

Amateur Architecture Studio

WANG Shu

Partner
LU Wenyu

Established Gegründet
1998

Awards Preise

2004	China Architectural Art Award
2006	Holcim Foundation Award for Asian-Pacific Sustainable Construction, Zurich
2007	SFA Award, Global Sustainable Construction
2007	Global Award for Sustainability Finalist, Paris
2008	International High-rise Award Nominee, Frankfurt/Main

Important Projects Wichtige Projekte

2003–2008	Ningbo History Museum, Ningbo
2002–2007	New academy campus of China Academy of Art in Hangzhou
2001–2005	Ningbo Art Museum, Ningbo
2006	Tiles Garden, Venice Architecture Biennale, Italy
2003–2006	Five Scattered Houses, Ningbo
2003–2006	Ceramic House, Jinhua
2002–2007	Vertical Housing, Hangzhou

01 Ceramic House, Jinhua City

Location Standort: Jinhua City, Zhejiang

Program Raumprogramm: Café

Architect Architekt: WANG Shu

Ceramic artist Keramikkünstler: ZHOU Wu

Client Bauherr: Jinhua City Government

Design Entwurf: 2004

Construction Ausführung: 2005–2006

Site area Fläche Baugrundstück: 130 m²

Gross floor area Bruttogeschossfläche: approx. 130 m²

Photographer Fotograf: LV Hengzhong

Ceramic House, a small 100 square-meter café, is Building No.9 of Jinhua Art and Architecture Park, developed by Jinhua city government as a riverbank green belt. The architect decided to make it a ceramic product, resembling a Song Dynasty ink basin, yet incorporating both wind and water. The single-story building borrows the shape of an ink basin, its front facing south and the rear facing north. When drinking coffee inside, one feels as if sitting at the bottom of the ink basin. A ramp to the northwest redirects the southeastern breeze. As there are high levels of precipitation in Jinhua, the rainwater drains directly along the ramp from northwest to southeast; the top of the ramp has been planted with several large trees. It is quite thought-provoking to sit inside and look up; at one point along the ramp all evidence of perspective appears to be lost. The east and the west façades are designed with many small openings, which apart from being functional, for daylight and ventilation purposes, also indicate the orientation of the building.

The usable interior space is about ninety square meters, and the cantilevered spaces to the north and the south comprise about forty square meters. Access to the roof, which opens to a magnificent view of the river, is via the west gate. All interior and exterior walls are covered in ceramic tiles designed by the ceramic artist ZHOU Wu, making the building colorful. The irregularly colored walls and spotted ceramics reverberate with a building located to the east designed by Ai Weiwei and one to the west by DING Yi.

Das Ceramic House, ein kleines Café von 100 Quadratmetern, ist Gebäude Nr. 9 des Jinhua Art and Architecture Park, der von der Stadtregierung Jinhua als Grüngürtel am Flussufer angelegt wurde. Der Architekt entschied sich für ein „Keramikobjekt", ähnlich einer Tintenschale der Songdynastie, das die Themen Wind und Wasser evoziert. Das eingeschossige Gebäude macht sich die Form der Tintenschale zu eigen, wobei die Front nach Süden und die Rückfassade nach Norden ausgerichtet sind. Beim Kaffeetrinken fühlt man sich wie auf dem Boden dieser Tintenschale. Ein rampenförmiger Hof nach Nordwesten nimmt die südöstliche Brise auf und lässt den in Jinhua häufigen Regen abfließen. Am Kopf der Rampe wurden einige große Bäume gepflanzt. Im Inneren zu sitzen und die Rampe hinaufzublicken, ist ein kontemplatives Erlebnis: Auf einmal scheint sich jede Perspektive entlang des Blicks zu verlieren. Viele kleine Öffnungen in den Ost- und Westfassaden markieren neben ihrer Funktion für die Belichtung und Belüftung auch die Ausrichtung des Gebäudes.

Die Nutzfläche des Innenraums umfasst etwa 90 Quadratmeter und die auskragenden Flächen im Süden und Norden noch einmal etwa 40 Quadratmeter. Über das Westtor gelangt man auf eine Dachterrasse mit herrlichem Blick auf den Fluss. Alle Innen- und Außenwandflächen sind mit Keramikfliesen des Keramikkünstlers ZHOU Wu bedeckt, was dem Gebäude Farbigkeit verleiht. Die unregelmäßigen Farben der Wände und die bunt gefleckte Keramik korrespondieren mit dem Gebäude von Ai Weiwei im Osten und dem von DING Yi im Westen.

1	South terrace Südterrasse
2	West gate Westtor
3	Ground floor plan Grundriss Erdgeschoss
4	Ramp from north Rampe von Norden
5	Ramp facing north Rampe Richtung Norden

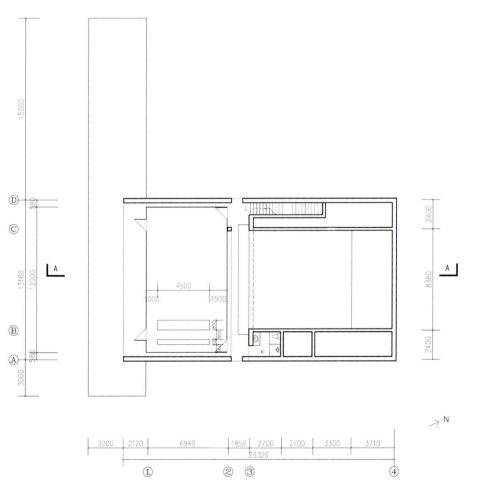

24 Amateur Architecture Studio

02 China Academy of Art, New Campus of Xiangshan School, Hangzhou

Location Standort: Hangzhou, Zhejiang

Program Raumprogramm: School Hochschule

Architectural team Architektenteam: WANG Shu, LU Wenyu

Client Bauherr: China Academy of Art

Design Entwurf: 2001 (first phase); 2004 (second phase)

Construction Ausführung: 2004 (1st phase); 2007 (2nd phase)

Site area Fläche Baugrundstück: 266,640 m²

Gross floor area Bruttogeschossfläche: 150,000 m²

Photographer Fotograf: LV Hengzhong

Xiangshan campus is part of a new extension to the China Academy of Fine Arts, intended to accommodate more than 500 members of staff and 5,000 students.

In 2000, the academy decided that its new extension should be located on the eastern tip of the south Hangzhou Mountains rather than in a government-zoned higher education district; according to Chinese tradition, natural landscape is more important than architecture itself when it comes to choosing the perfect site for education.

The site surrounds a fifty-meter high hill named "Xiang." Two small streams flow down from the mountains in the west, around the northern and the southern sides of the hill, to merge to its east before continuing into the Qiantang River. Historically, traditional Chinese academic buildings were situated in garden courtyards, however the new Xiangshan campus has been developed around a series of topographically diverse courtyards built to harmonize with the hill. The buildings rotate in sensitive response to the mountains and rivers. Existing farmlands, streams and fishponds have been protected. Intricate and poetic spaces associated with classical Chinese gardens have been innovatively transformed into something resembling large-scale pastoral simplicity.

In response to extensive demolitions and reconstructions taking place in China, more than seven million pieces of bricks and roof tiles from different decades were salvaged from demolition sites all over Zhejiang province to build this new campus. Bricks and tiles, which would otherwise have been dumped, were reused; Chinese vernacular sustainable construction also reappears here.

Der Xiangshan Campus ist Teil einer neuen Erweiterung für die China Academy of Fine Arts, die mehr als 500 Mitarbeiter und 5000 Studenten beherbergen soll.

Im Jahr 2000 entschied die Akademie, dass ihre Erweiterung eher am Fuß der Berge südlich von Hangzhou als in einem von der Regierung ausgewiesenen Universitätsbezirk liegen sollte. Denn laut chinesischer Tradition spielt die landschaftliche Einbettung bei der Auswahl des perfekten Standorts für eine Schule eine größere Rolle als die Architektur selbst.

Das Grundstück umgibt den 50 Meter hohen Hügel Xiangshan. Aus den Bergen im Westen entspringen zwei kleine Flüsse, jeweils nördlich und südlich des Hügels, die östlich des Hügels zusammentreffen, bevor sie in den Fluss Qiantang fließen. Traditionell werden akademische Gebäude in China in Gartenhöfe platziert, aber der neue Xiangshan Campus wurde um eine Reihe von Höfen unterschiedlicher Topografie herum entworfen, die sich auf den Hügel beziehen. Die Gebäude richten sich einfühlsam an den Bergen und Flüssen aus. Bestehende landwirtschaftliche Flächen, Flüsse und Fischteiche wurden geschützt. Die Komplexität und Poesie chinesischer Gärten wurden innovativ in eine Art großmaßstäbliche Landidylle übertragen.

Als Reaktion auf die umfassenden Zerstörungen und Umbauten, die in China an der Tagesordnung sind, wurden mehr als sieben Millionen Backsteine und Dachziegel von Abbruchstellen aus der gesamten Provinz Zhejiang geborgen, um diesen neuen Campus zu errichten. Mauerwerk und Ziegel, die sonst entsorgt worden wären, sind somit wiederverwendet worden. Auch in diesem Sinne entsteht alltägliche chinesische Architektur hier neu.

1 Exterior view with bamboo façade panels
  Ansicht mit Bambusfassadenpaneelen
2 Building No.11 from west
  Haus 11 von Westen
3 Site of phase II, Xiangshan campus
  Lageplan Phase II Xiangshan Campus
4 Bird's eye view of building No.19 from the west
  Haus 19, Vogelperspektive von Westen

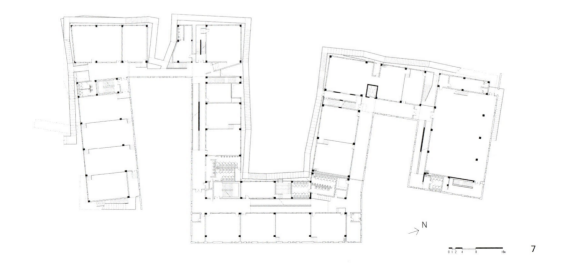

5	West view of building No.11 Westansicht von Haus 11
6, 8	Corridors inside building No.11 Flure im Haus 11
7	Plan of building No.11 Grundriss von Haus 11
9	East elevation of building No.11 Ostansicht von Haus 11
10	West elevation of building No.11 Westansicht von Haus 11
11	South elevation of building No.11 Südansicht von Haus 11
12	North elevation of building No.11 Nordansicht von Haus 11

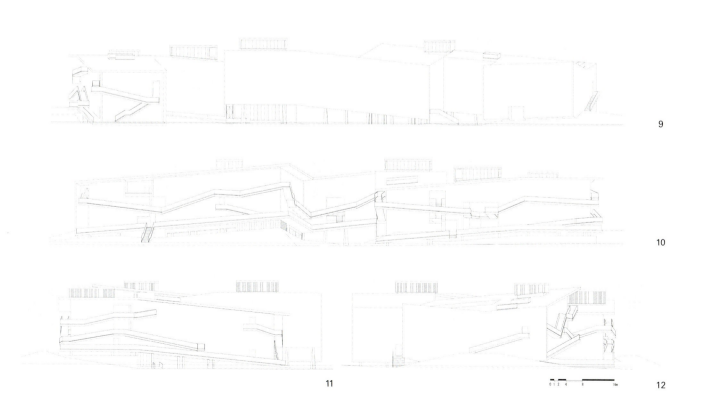

Ningbo History Museum, Ningbo

Location Standort: Ningbo, Zhejiang

Program Raumprogramm: Museum

Architectural team Architektenteam: WANG Shu, LU Wenyu

Client Bauherr: Ningbo History Museum

Design Entwurf: 2003–2005

Construction Ausführung: 2006–2008

Site area Fläche Baugrundstück: 45,333 m²

Gross floor area Bruttogeschossfläche: 30,000 m²

Photographer Fotograf: LV Hengzhong

The site involves a flat area situated against a background of distant mountains; urbanization has expanded to this area. A new master plan stipulates that an isolated object be designed by the architects, who have come up with the idea of an artificial mountain with foundations in Chinese tradition. The base of the structure is a simple box. As it rises, the box explodes into a mountainous form. Visitors can access the museum via an oval cave spanning thirty meters. The internal structure consists of three "valleys," each with an escalator; one is exterior while the other two connect the interior spaces. Four caves have been arranged at the entrance, the lobby and the "cliffs" of the exterior "valley." Two sunken courtyards dominate the center while two more discreet ones are hidden further inside.

A mountainous topography has been superimposed. Multiple paths, which rise from ground level up into a labyrinth of pathways, interconnect public spaces. This layout is particularly flexible in accommodating ever-changing exhibitions. From interior to exterior, the structure has been covered by bamboo-cast concrete and more than twenty types of miscellaneous recycled bricks and roof tiles. Suspended between the natural and the artificial, provocative yet austere, this structure expresses only the rawness of the mountains. The north wing rests within an artificial body of water with reed-covered banks. Water flows over a dam at the middle entrance, ending at a large field of cobblestones. A generous balcony extrudes from behind the middle section, peering through four cracks into the city, the rice fields and the distant mountains.

Das Grundstück liegt auf einer Ebene vor dem Hintergrund entfernter Berge, auf die sich die Stadt ausgedehnt hat. Das solitäre Bauwerk, das der Bebauungsplan vorsieht, regte die Architekten dazu an, ein künstliches Felsmassiv zu entwerfen, das – im wahrsten Sinne des Wortes – in den chinesischen Traditionen wurzelt. Das Gebäude geht von einer einfachen Box aus: Mit zunehmender Höhe „explodiert" sie zu einer felsigen Form. Die Besucher gelangen über eine 30 Meter lange ovale „Höhle" in das Museum. Das Innere wird von drei „Tälern" strukturiert, die jeweils über Rolltreppen erschlossen sind. Am Eingang, der Lobby und den steil aufragenden Wänden des äußeren Tals liegen vier „Höhlen". Zwei abgesenkte Höfe bilden das Zentrum des Baus, zwei weitere liegen tiefer im Inneren verborgen.

Dem Ganzen wurde eine bergige Topografie übergestülpt. Verschiedene Pfade, die sich vom Erdgeschoss aus labyrinthisch verzweigen, verbinden die öffentlichen Räume. Der Entwurf ist aufgrund seiner Flexibilität für die ständig wechselnden Ausstellungen besonders geeignet. Von innen nach außen ist das Bauwerk mit bambusverschaltem Beton und über 20 verschiedenen Arten wiederverwendeter Backsteine und Ziegel verkleidet. Im Spannungsfeld zwischen Künstlichem und Natürlichem – provokativ und doch streng – bezieht sich dieses Gebäude auf die Rauheit der Berge. Der nördliche Flügel liegt in einem künstlichen Wasserbecken mit Reetufern. Wasser fließt am Mitteleingang über einen Damm zu einem großen Geröllfeld. Hinter dem Mittelteil ragt ein großzügiger Balkon hervor, der durch vier Durchbrüche Blicke auf die Stadt, die Reisfelder und die fernen Berge gewährt.

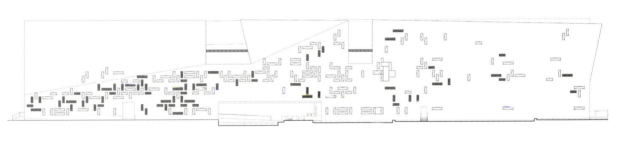

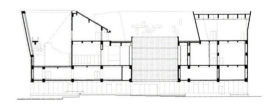

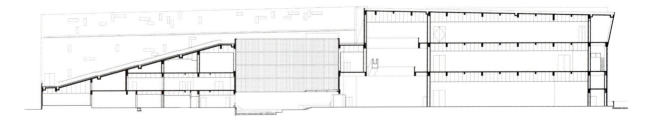

34　Amateur Architecture Studio

1 Main façade Hauptfassade
2 View from north-east
  Blick von Nordosten
3 West elevation Westansicht
4 South elevation Südansicht
5 Cross section Querschnitt
6 Longitudinal section Längsschnitt
7 View from west Blick von Westen
8 Exhibition hall Ausstellungshalle
9 Passageway beside restaurant
  Passage neben Restaurant

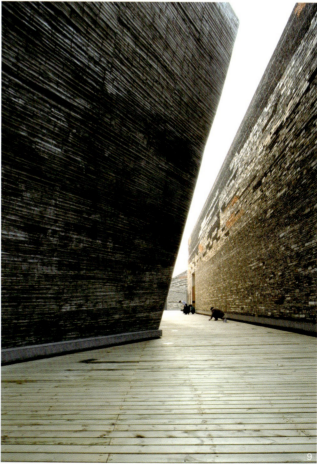

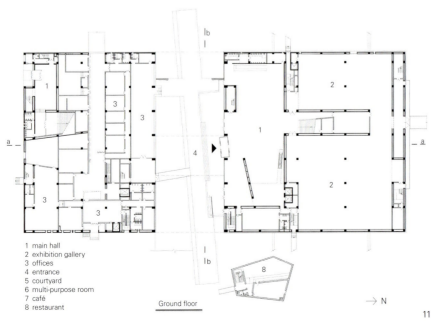

1 main hall
2 exhibition gallery
3 offices
4 entrance
5 courtyard
6 multi-purpose room
7 café
8 restaurant

Ground floor

→ N

11

36 Amateur Architecture Studio

10 Courtyard beside restaurant
   Hof neben Restaurant
11 Ground floor plan Grundriss Ergeschoss
12 View down ramp Blick die Rampe hinunter

Atelier Z+
2B 568 Ou'yang Road
200081 Shanghai
Phone +86 21 5666 5987
Fax +86 21 5666 7295
atelier_zplus@163.com

Atelier Z+

ZHANG Bin
ZHOU Wei

Established Gegründet
2002

Awards Preise

2004	WA Chinese Award / Honorable Mentions
2006	Architectural Society of China, Architectural Creation Award
2006	Architectural Society of China, Young Architects Awards
2006	Architectural Society of Shanghai, Architectural Creation Award
2006	Architectural Society of Shanghai, Architectural Creation Award
2008	Business Week / Architectural Record China Awards / Best Public Projects, New York
2008	Architectural Society of China, Architectural Creation Award

Important Projects Wichtige Projekte

2007	Shanghai Culture and Information Industry Park, First Phase, Malu, Jiading, Shanghai
2007-2009	Culture and Sports Centre, Anting, Jiading, Shanghai
2006-2007	Liangtang Town Hall, Qingpu
2005-2007	Court Houses, Second Phase, Tianya Waterscape Town, Suzhou
2004-2006	Sino-French Centre, Tongji-University, Shanghai
2002-2004	Building C, College of Architecture and Urban Planning, Tongji University, Shanghai

04 Liantang Town Hall, Shanghai

Location Standort: Qingpu, Shanghai

Program Raumprogramm: Office Büros

Architectural team Architektenteam: ZHANG Bin, ZHOU Wei

Client Bauherr: The People's Government of Liantang Town, Qingpu, Shanghai

Design Entwurf: 2006

Construction Ausführung: 2008–2009

Site area Fläche Baugrundstück: 23,590 m^2

Gross building area Bruttogeschossfläche: 5,450 m^2

Photographer Fotograf: Atelier Z+

This project is a new governmental office building for Liantang, a canal town located to the southwest of Qingpu, Shanghai. It continues the development of the town, exploring the art of inheriting and updating the internal structures of traditional local architecture. It must accommodate various functions to satisfy both public and private demand. This requires breaking through the scale restrictions of traditional courtyard space by applying a combination of a variety and flexibility of scales. A major courtyard is located at the center of this building, which is of multiple-courtyard structure, and smaller courtyards of different functions are dispersed around it. These independent courtyards are harmoniously characterized by diverse spatial features, which creates a pleasant working environment. A three-story main office building, structured in two rows, is located adjacent to the southern square. The ground floor of the southern half is partly elevated, opening the entrance courtyard between the two building parts to the square. The double-height gallery on the second floor provides the main building's framework, while four independent office units and three vertical gardens in the southern block create small pockets of space. A community service center is located to the east and a conference center and cafeteria to the north while there is a veranda opposite the main courtyard in the south. Offices are situated in the west directly under the town council, forming three intertwining courtyards that are connected to the canal through a pierced tracery wall. A library and a recreational room are located in the main courtyard, like a bright pavilion which separates it into two distinct areas. The building presents an image of a continuous courtyard structure characterized by white walls and single-sloped, black-tiled roofs. The delicate details called for appropriate materials, the tectonics of local style, and practicable creativity.

Dieser Neubau eines staatlichen Verwaltungsgebäudes im Rahmen des Stadtentwicklungsprogramms für Liantang, eine Kanalstadt südwestlich von Qingpu, Shanghai, widmet sich der Kunst des Bewahrens und Weiterführens der gewachsenen Strukturen traditioneller, lokaler Architektur. Um den unterschiedlichen öffentlichen und privaten Anforderungen gerecht zu werden, war es nötig, die maßstäbliche Beschränkung traditioneller Hofarchitektur zu überwinden und stattdessen unterschiedliche, flexibel ausgelegte Maßstäbe zu kombinieren. Ein großer, zentraler Hof wird von vielen kleineren Höfen unterschiedlicher Funktion umgeben, deren Ausstattung zu einer angenehmen Arbeitsatmosphäre beiträgt. Ein in zwei Flügel aufgeteiltes, dreigeschossiges Bürogebäude liegt direkt am südlichen Vorplatz. Das Erdgeschoss des Südflügels ist dabei teilweise aufgeständert, um so den Eingangshof zwischen den beiden Flügeln zum Platz hin zu öffnen. Die zweigeschossige Galerie im zweiten Stock durchzieht das gesamte Gebäude; im Südflügel teilen vier unabhängige Bürotrakte und drei vertikale Gärten den Raum in kleinere Einheiten auf. Ein Bürgerzentrum ist im Osten angeschlossen, im Norden ein Konferenzzentrum und eine Cafeteria mit südlicher, zum Haupthof orientierter Veranda. Direkt unter den Räumen des Stadtrats im Westen umgeben Büros drei zusammenhängende Höfe, die über ein transparentes Wandgitter zum Kanal hin orientiert sind. Ein lichter Pavillon mit einer Bibliothek und einem Freizeitraum teilt den Haupthof. Das Gebäude bildet eine durchgängige Hofstruktur, die von weißen Wänden und schwarz gedeckten Pultdächern geprägt ist. Die feinen Details sind in angemessenen Materialien ausgeführt und zeugen von lokaler Baukunst sowie praxisnaher Kreativität.

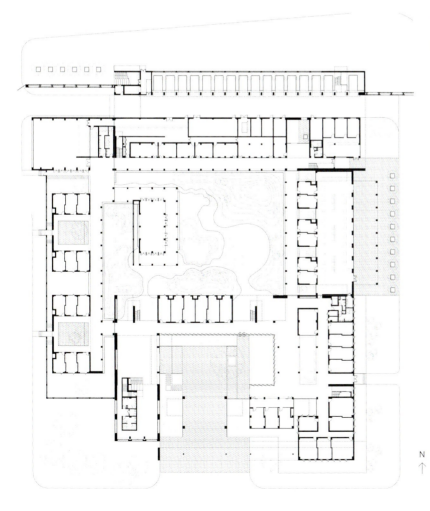

1 Rendering bird's eye view from south-west
Rendering Vogelperspektive von Südwesten
2 Ground floor plan Grundriss Erdgeschoss

41

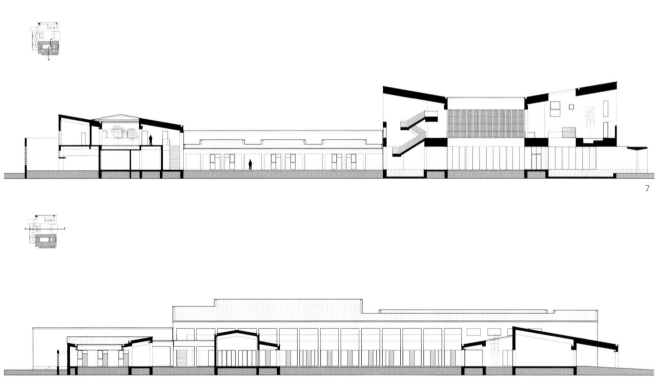

3 View from the south-east Südostansicht
4 View from the north-east Nordostansicht
5 Hall Halle
6 Roof garden Dachgarten
7 Section north-south Schnitt Nord-Süd
8 Section east-west Schnitt Ost-West

05 Building C, College of Architecture and Urban Planning, Tongji University, Shanghai

Location Standort: Tongji University, Shanghai

Program Raumprogramm: Research Forschung

Architectural team Architektenteam: ZHANG Bin, ZHOU Wei

Client Bauherr: Tongji University

Design Entwurf: 2002–2004

Construction Ausführung: 2002–2004

Site area Fläche Baugrundstück: 4,140 m²

Gross building area Bruttogeschossfläche: 1,485 m²

Photographer Fotograf: Atelier Z+

This project is programmed for research and graduate student education. It is located on a congested site, adjoining an existing main building and the campus enclosing wall. It is intended to expose the "dormant" potential of this silent corner in the campus and of the students themselves. The space was designed to form a sort of flowing continuum; the tedium of service and serviced space is broken as communication space becomes the main component and functional space the "plug and play" element.

The core of this building is articulated by a central east to west connecting corridor system with a straight staircase linking all floors of working spaces and a series of vertical light shafts. Research workshops fill the main body of the building, occupying the southern side of the corridor on all of the upper floors. Supervisors' studios, adaptable workshops and vertical circulation service units are arranged within two volumes, which plug in at different heights to the north of the corridor, incorporating three overlapping voids. They share a common transparent glass envelope on the north facade. A waterfall and stepped planting in the sunken garden to the south provide the underground gallery with a vivid recreational space. The overlapping of large-scale public space from north to south produces intense variation in spatial dimension and orientation, intertwining inside with outside. The architects strived to emphasize visibility within the interior spaces as well as the expressivity of surface materials, rather than focusing on the unity of the exterior façade. The diverse spatial types have been distinguished in the form and materiality of the façade, allowing each surface of the building to respond to a different context within the site.

Dieses Projekt liegt auf einem sehr dicht bebauten Areal und grenzt an das bestehende Hauptgebäude und die den Campus umgebende Mauer im Norden. Es soll diesen stillen Winkel des Campus – und die Studierenden selbst – aus dem „Dornröschenschlaf" wecken. Der Entwurf schafft ein fließendes Raumkontinuum; die Alltäglichkeit eines Funktionsgebäudes wird aufgebrochen, indem der kommunikative Raum in den Vordergrund gerückt wird, nach dem „plug and play"-Prinzip durch Funktionsräume ergänzt.

Das innere Rückgrat dieses Gebäudes wird durch ein von Osten nach Westen verlaufendes Korridorsystem mit einläufiger Treppe, die alle Geschosse und Arbeitsbereiche erschließt, und eine Reihe vertikaler Lichtschächte artikuliert. Das Gebäude wird vorrangig von Forschungswerkstätten belegt, die südlich des Korridors auf allen Obergeschossen liegen. Die Studios der Lehrenden, flexible Werkstätten und vertikale Erschließung sind in zwei Baukörpern angeordnet, die auf der Nordseite auf unterschiedlichen Geschossen an das Rückgrat andocken und auch drei überlappende Lufträume einschließen. Sie werden durch eine gemeinsame transparente Glashülle im Norden verbunden. Ein Wasserfall und stufenförmige Bepflanzung im südlichen Senkgarten bilden einen lebendigen Freizeitbereich im Untergeschoss. Indem sich große öffentliche Bereiche von Norden nach Süden überlappen, variieren Dimensionen und Orientierung der Räume, Innen und Außen durchdringen sich. Die Architekten wollten eher die Transparenz im Innenraum und die Expressivität der Oberflächenmaterialien betonen, als sich auf die Durchgängigkeit der Außenfassade zu konzentrieren. Die verschiedenen Raumtypen sind in Form und Material in der Fassade abgebildet, sodass die Außenhaut des Gebäudes unterschiedlich auf den jeweiligen Umgebungskontext reagiert.

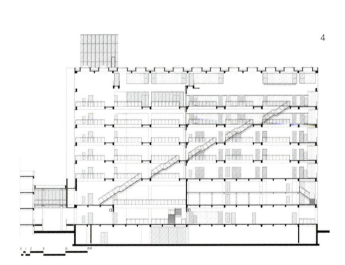
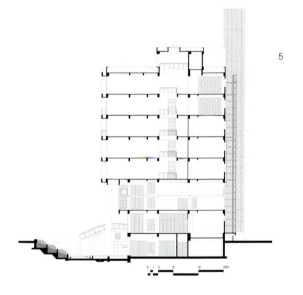
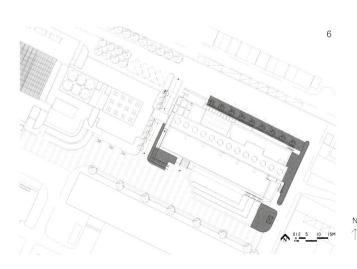

1. View from the south-west
   Südwestansicht
2. Seventh floor roof garden
   7. Obergeschoss, Dachgarten
3. Main staircase Haupttreppe
4. Longitudinal section Längsschnitt
5. North-south cross-section
   Nord-Süd-Querschnitt
6. Site plan Lageplan
7. Entrance Eingang

8	Seventh floor central corridor
	Flur 7. Obergeschoss
9	First floor plan
	Grundriss 1. Obergeschoss
10	Stairwell Treppenhaus
11	Axonometry Axonometrie
12	Third floor atrium
	Atrium im 3. Obergeschoss

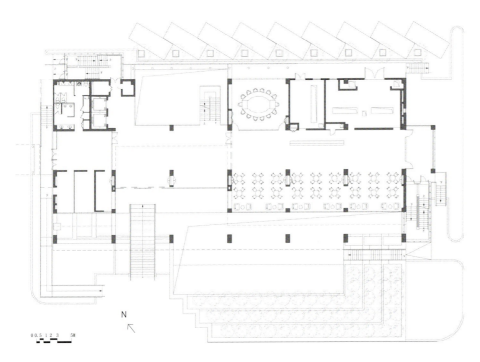

48   Atelier Z+

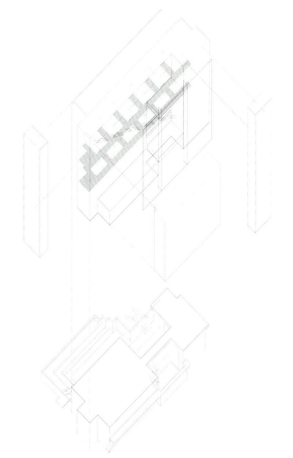

06 Sino-French Center, Tongji University, Shanghai

Location Standort: Main Campus of Tongji University, Shanghai

Program Raumprogramm: School Hochschule

Architectural team Architektenteam: ZHOU Wei, ZHANG Bin

Client Bauherr: Tongji University

Design Entwurf: 2004–2006

Construction Ausführung: 2004–2006

Site area Fläche Baugrundstück: 9,204 m²

Gross building area Bruttogeschossfläche: 3,142 m²

Photographer Fotograf: ZHANG Siye

This project is located on the southeastern corner of the campus, neighboring the oldest existing building. Preconditions for the building were that the XuRi Building, located on the northwestern corner of the site, be preserved and that all trees on the site be retained. The goal of this project was to create a formal system which would integrate the program, the context of the site and the cultural context. The architects used a geometrical diagram to define the program and circulation, to conform to site restrictions, and symbolically to represent cultural exchange between the two countries. Their "hand in hand" diagram was used to organize the whole building with its inherent structure of dualistic juxtaposition.

The program is composed of three parts: classrooms, offices, and public gathering space. Two similar but diverse zigzag volumes, occupied by the college and office sector respectively, overlap and intertwine; they are linked underground and on the upper level by a public space volume. The classroom and office sectors share the main entrance, which is located in a void in the intersection of their two volumes. The public gathering space has its own lobby, which faces onto a roof pool and a sunken garden; it connects underground to an exhibition hall and to a lecture hall on the upper level. The regular shape of most of the units expresses the functionality of the college and offices. Yet the zigzag corridor that connects these units creates abundant interest within the inside and outside spaces. Varying materials and tectonics have been applied to the different components of this complex.

Vorgabe für dieses Projekt am südöstlichen Ende des Campus, neben dem ältesten bestehenden Bau, war die Erhaltung des XuRi-Gebäudes am nordwestlichen Ende und aller Bäume auf dem Gelände. Der Entwurf musste dem Raumprogramm genügen, aber auch Ort und kulturellen Bezug berücksichtigen. Um den besonderen Bedingungen des Grundstücks gerecht zu werden und um den kulturellen Austausch zwischen China und Frankreich zu symbolisieren, benutzten die Architekten ein geometrisches Schaubild, das „Hand in Hand"-Diagramm. Das hier versinnbildlichte Prinzip der Gegenüberstellung bestimmt die Organisation des gesamten Gebäudes.

Das Raumprogramm besteht aus drei Teilen: Seminarräumen, Büros und kommunaler Raum. Zwei ähnliche zickzackförmige Baukörper, die jeweils von dem Seminar- und Büroblock besetzt werden, überlappen und durchdringen sich. Sie sind im Untergeschoss und im Obergeschoss durch den kommunalen Raum verbunden. Die Seminar- und Bürobereiche nutzen denselben Haupteingang, der in einem Spalt zwischen den beiden Baukörpern liegt. Der kommunale Raum besitzt seine eigene Lobby, die zu einem Dachwasserbecken und einem tiefer gelegenen Garten hin ausgerichtet sind. Er schließt im Untergeschoss an eine Ausstellungshalle und einen Vorlesungssaal im Obergeschoss an. Die regelmäßigen Formen der meisten Bauteile spiegeln die Funktionalität der Schule und der Büros. Dennoch bringt der verbindende Korridor Abwechslung im Innen- und Außenbereich. Die Bauteile weisen jeweils unterschiedliche Materialien und Fügungen auf.

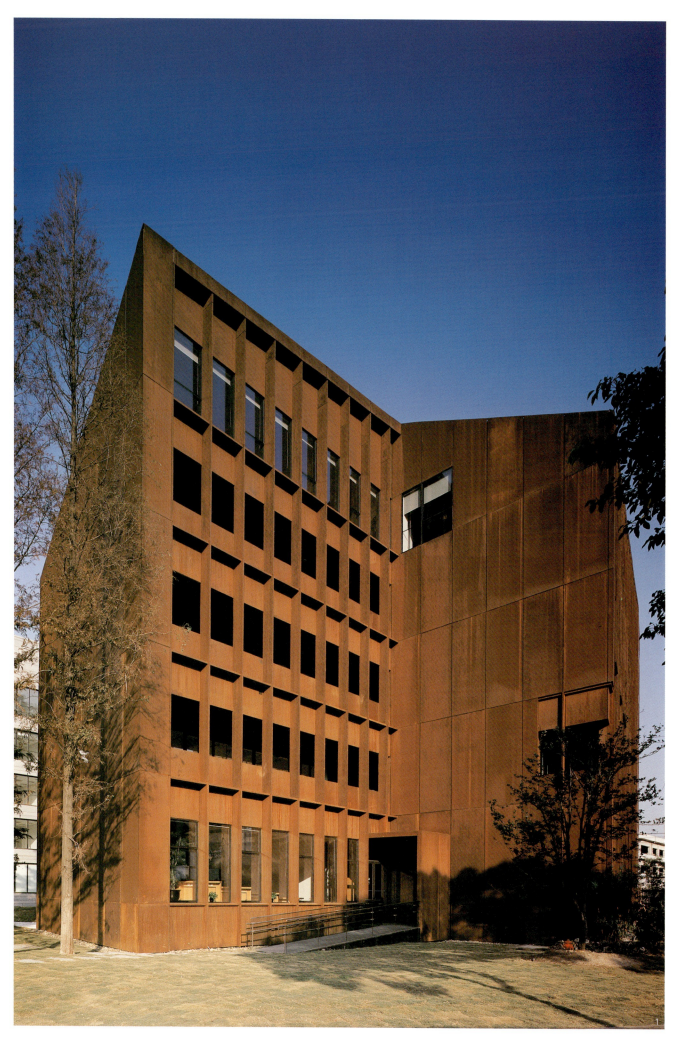

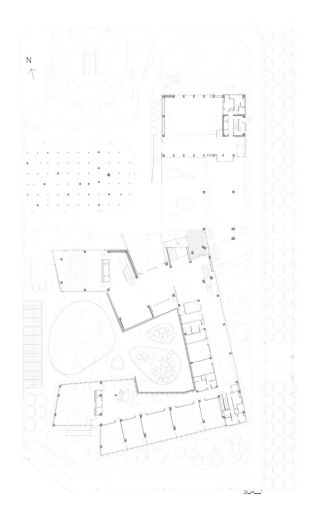

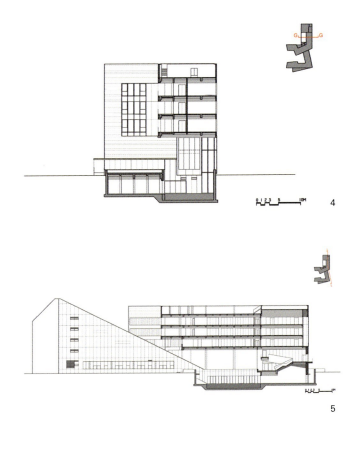

52 Atelier Z+

1 View from south-west Südwestansicht
2 Main entrance Haupteingang
3 Ground floor plan Grundriss Erdgeschoss
4 Cross section Querschnitt
5 Longitudinal section Längsschnitt
6 Stair of college sector Treppe im College
7 Sunken garden Tiefhof

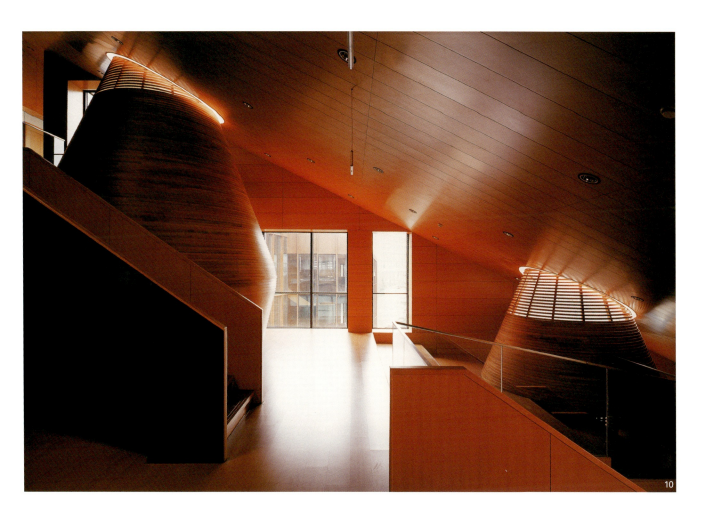

8	Lecture hall Vorlesungssaal
9, 10	Interior of office sector Innenräume Büroflügel
11	Axonometry Axonometrie

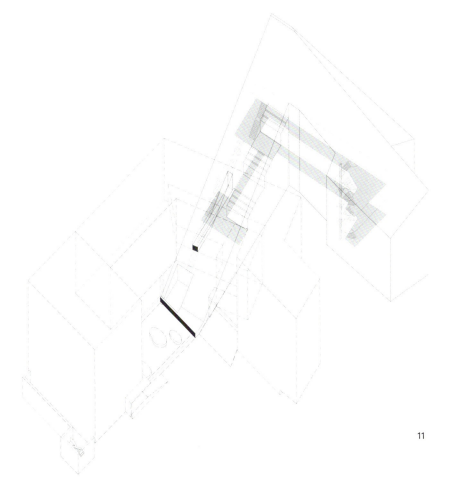

DnA_Design and Architecture
Liang ma jia yuan 36-4-2103, Nan shi li
ju, Jiu xian qiao Road Chaoyang District,
Beijing
Phone +8610 6433 2175
Fax +8610 6433 2175
www.designandarchitecture.net
DnA_beijing@126.com

DnA_Design and Architecture

XU Tiantian

Established Gegründet
2004

Awards Preise

2008	Architecture League, Young Architects Award, New York
2008	WA China Architecture Awards, Beijing
2008	AR Award Honorable Mention, London

Important Projects Wichtige Projekte

2009	Aquatic Center, Dalian
2007-2008	Songzhuang Artists' Residence, Beijing
2007-	Xixi Leisure Center, Zhejiang
2007-	Wushanzhuan Art Museum, Chengdu
2007-	Changbaishan 3 Public Activity, Jilin
2006-2009	Villa By Water, Inner Mongolia
2006-2007	Ordos Art Museum, Inner Mongolia
2005-2006	Songzhuang Art Center, Beijing

07 Songzhuang Artists' Residence, Beijing

Location Standort: Songzhuang, Beijing

Program Raumprogramm: Art studios Künstlerateliers

Architect Architekt: XU Tiantian

Client Bauherr: Private Privat

Design Entwurf: 2007–2009

Construction Ausführung: 2008–2009

Site area Fläche Baugrundstück: approx. 1,400 m²

Gross building area Bruttogeschossfläche: 5,300 m²

Photographer Fotograf: Savoye/ZHOU Ruogu

Located right next to the east sixth ring road of Beijing city, Songzhuang Artist Village is undergoing a dramatic expansion of its artistic population, increasing the demand for artist working and living space. A twenty-unit artists' residence facing a fishpond on a former outdoor storage lot is one of the local developments to target this demand.

The programmatic requirements of working and living define the height and geometry of both volumes: six-meter height for working and three-meter for living; a simple rectangular box as a studio and a more complex volume for living, incorporating bedroom, kitchen and toilet. The living volume is plugged into the working volume; either on the same level or via a staircase to an upper level.

The twenty units are regarded as containers stacked on this former industrial outdoor storage lot, creating expressive configuration and spatial quality. The interplay of volume and void, light and shadow allows artists and visitors to constantly explore and experiment with the outdoor communal space. It can be used for artistic production and presentation as well as linking the twenty units as twenty individual showrooms on open studio days. In other words, this complex is an alternative museum for the living creation of art and for exhibitions.

Die Einwohnerzahl der Künstlerkolonie Songzhuang an der östlichen sechsten Ringstraße von Peking steigt explosionsartig an, Arbeits- und Wohnräume für die Künstler werden knapp. Ein Künstlerwohnheim mit 20 Einheiten auf einem früheren Lagerplatz gegenüber einem Fischteich gehört zu den Maßnahmen, um diesem Bedarf abzuhelfen.

Das auf Wohnen und Arbeiten zugeschnittene Raumprogramm bestimmt Höhe und Geometrie beider Raummodule: sechs Meter Höhe für das Arbeiten und drei Meter für das Wohnen – eine einfache rechtwinklige Kiste als Studio und ein komplexerer Baukörper als Wohnung einschließlich Schlafzimmer, Küche und Toilette. Das Wohnvolumen dockt an den Arbeitsbaukörper an – entweder auf gleicher Ebene oder über eine Treppe zu erreichen.

Die 20 Einheiten gleichen Containern, die auf diesem vormaligen industriellen Lagerplatz aufgestapelt sind und erzeugen eine expressive Konfiguration und räumliche Qualität. Das Zusammenspiel von Körper und Leerraum, Licht und Schatten gestattet es Künstlern wie Besuchern, den gemeinschaftlichen Außenraum ständig neu zu entdecken und mit ihm zu experimentieren. Er kann für die künstlerische Produktion und Präsentation benutzt werden und die einzelnen Einheiten können an „Tagen des offenen Studios" sogar als 20 individuelle Galerien zusammengeschaltet werden. Mit anderen Worten: Dieser Komplex ist ein alternatives Museum für die lebendige Gestaltung und Präsentation von Kunst.

1 Exterior view Außenansicht
2 Ground floor plan Grundriss Erdgeschoss
3 First floor plan Grundriss 1. Obergeschoss
4 Second floor plan Grundriss 2. Obergeschoss
5 Third floor plan Grundriss 3. Obergeschoss

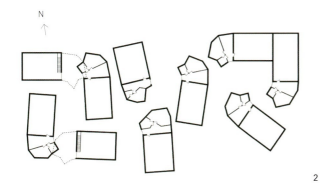

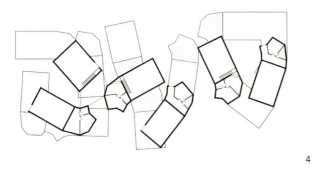
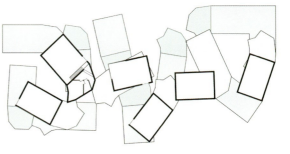

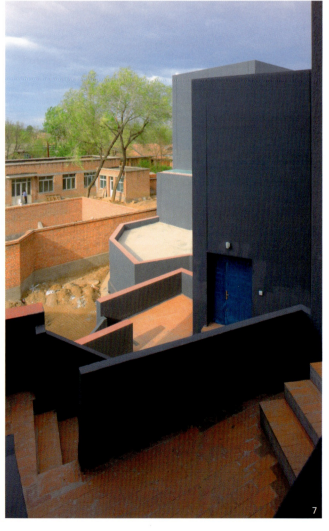

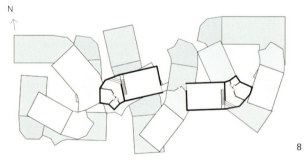

6	Exterior view Außenansicht
7, 9	Exterior details Fassadendetails
8	Fourth floor plan Grundriss 4. Obergeschoss

08 Ordos Art Museum, Inner Mongolia

Location Standort: **Ordos, Inner Mongolia** Innere Mongolei

Program Raumprogramm: **Museum**

Architectural team Architektenteam: **XU Tiantian, Guillaume Aubry, CHEN Yingnan**

Client Bauherr: **Jiangyuan Water Conservancy Construction Co., Ltd. Erdos.**

Design Entwurf: **2005–2006**

Construction Ausführung: **2006–2007**

Site area Fläche Baugrundstück: **4,200 m²**

Gross building area Bruttogeschossfläche: **2,700 m²**

Photographer Fotograf: **Savoye/ZHOU Ruogu**

The natural environment of the wild prairie of Erdos is an opportunity or rather a challenge to architects. As viewed from the project's concept map, there is no design, no label, no image, and even no symbolic meanings. The architect has simply placed a tortuous route through the wild land and put it into a box. Although the route is a little bit showy, its unadorned skin makes the architecture clear, which becomes the outstanding feature of this project.

Ordos Art Museum is the first building of Ordos' new civic center on a stretch of sand dunes along the lake that is dedicated as a "public corridor" with art and cultural facilities. This 2,700 square meters of exhibition and research space is distributed within an undulating form with a central span lifting clear off the ground, suggesting a desert viper winding over the dunes.

The space is conceived as one uninterrupted room with a series of openings absorbing natural light while offering cinematic views of the raw surroundings; the art exhibition mingles with the natural landscape, becoming an integrated experience for visitors.

Die wilde Prärielandschaft, die die Stadt Ordos in der Inneren Mongolei umgibt, stellt für Architekten eine Gelegenheit oder vielmehr eine Herausforderung dar. Wie man an den Konzeptzeichnungen des Projektes sehen kann, gibt es kein Design, kein Label, kein Sinnbild – noch nicht einmal symbolische Bedeutungen. Die Architektin hat einfach einen gewundenen Weg durch die Landschaft gezogen und diesen Weg eingehaust. Obwohl der Wegverlauf etwas prätentiös ist, verleiht ihm seine schnörkellose Haut doch die markante Klarheit, die dieses Projekt auszeichnet.

Das Ordos Art Museum ist das erste Gebäude von Ordos' Verwaltungszentrum auf Sanddünen entlang des Sees, an dem ein „öffentlicher Korridor" mit Kunst- und Kultureinrichtungen entstehen soll. Die Ausstellungs- und Forschungsfläche von 2700 Quadratmetern sind innerhalb einer sich windenden Form untergebracht, wobei sich ein zentraler Abschnitt deutlich vom Boden erhebt und an eine Wüstenviper erinnert, die sich über die Dünen schlängelt.

Der Raum ist als ein ununterbrochenes Volumen mit einer Reihe von Öffnungen für Tageslicht gedacht, die panoramaartige Ausblicke auf die wilde Landschaft eröffnen: Natur und Kunst verbinden sich für die Besucher zu einem ganzheitlichen Erlebnis.

1 Exterior view from south-east
Außenansicht von Südosten
2 Ground floor plan Grundriss Ergeschoss
3 First floor plan Grundriss 1. Obergeschoss

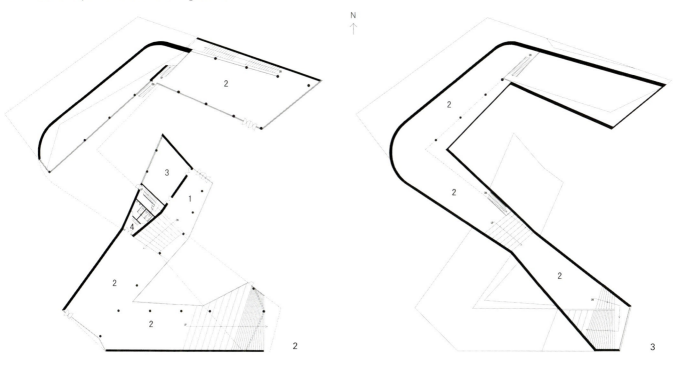

4 Exterior view from north-east
Außenansicht von Nordosten
5, 6 Façade details Fassadendetails

64　DnA_Design and Architecture

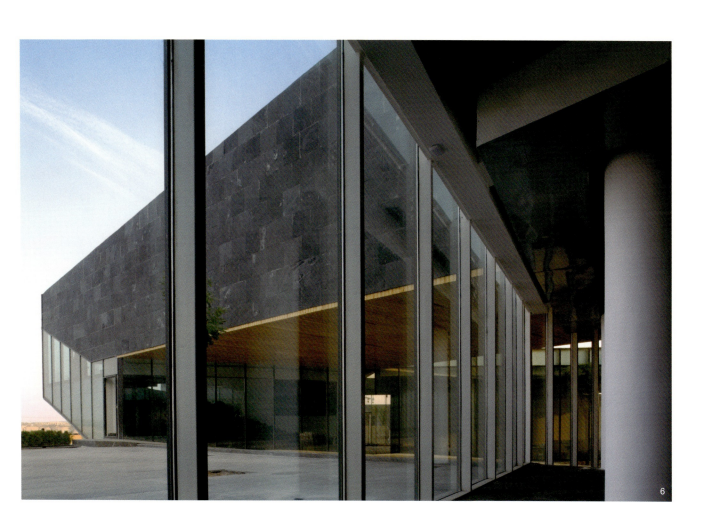

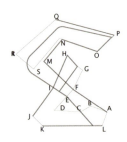

8

66 DnA_Design and Architecture

7 Exterior view Außenansicht
8 Elevation diagrams Ansicht Diagramme
9, 10 Interior view ramp Innenraum Rampe

Songzhuang Art Center, Beijing

Location Standort: **Songzhuang, Beijing**

Program Raumprogramm: **Museum**

Architectural team Architektenteam: **XU Tiantian, CHEN Yingnan, ZHU Junjie**

Client Bauherr: **Local government** Bezirksregierung

Design Entwurf: **2005–2006**

Construction Ausführung: **2005–2006**

Site area Fläche Baugrundstück: **6,000 m^2**

Gross building area Bruttogeschossfläche: **5,000 m^2**

Photographer Fotograf: **Savoye/ZHOU Ruogu**

Songzhuang Art Center is located in Xiaobo villiage, Songzhuang town, where around 4,000 artists live. It has become a well-recognized contemporary Chinese art village, only a forty-five-minute drive from Beijing. The project is the first public art facility to be built in this area; as an art center it provides a platform for the local community.

The design of this project, from exterior form to interior, including materials, is abstracted from the image of Xiaobo village. The architect emphasizes the harmonious co-existence between environment and architecture through simple architectural language and special attention to environment, space, structure and material aspects, thus promoting the mergence of contemporary aesthetics and local culture.

The exhibition space has been elevated to create a welcoming, horizontal, flowing, multi-purpose space on the ground level, to host exhibitions and events and as a casual common area. The second level is a rather introverted artistic space with light entering only from above and from the courtyard. The surrounding landscape does not necessarily intrude; art is the view here.

Das Songzhuang Art Center liegt im Dorf Xiaobo bei der Stadt Songzhuang, wo rund 4000 Künstler leben. Etwa 45 Minuten Fahrt von Pekings Zentrum entfernt, ist der Ort zu einem hochangesehenen Zentrum für zeitgenössische chinesische Kunst geworden. Das Projekt bildet die erste öffentliche Kunsteinrichtung in dieser Gegend und bietet der örtlichen Gemeinschaft eine Plattform.

Der Entwurf dieses Projekts spiegelt von der äußeren Form über die verwendeten Materialien bis ins Innere in abstrakter Form das alte Dorf Xiaobo wider. Die Architektin betont das harmonische Miteinander von Umwelt und Architektur durch eine einfache architektonische Sprache. Indem sie der Umgebung, dem Raum, der Konstruktion und dem Material besondere Aufmerksamkeit widmet, gelingt ihr die Verschmelzung von zeitgenössischer Ästhetik und lokaler Kultur.

Der Ausstellungsraum ist angehoben worden, um im Erdgeschoss einen einladenden, horizontalen, fließenden Mehrzweckraum für Ausstellungen und Veranstaltungen und als frei zugänglichen Bereich zu schaffen. Das Obergeschoss ist ein eher introvertierter künstlerischer Raum, in den Licht nur von oben und den Höfen eindringt. Die umgebende Landschaft bleibt eher draußen – der Fokus liegt hier eindeutig auf der Kunst.

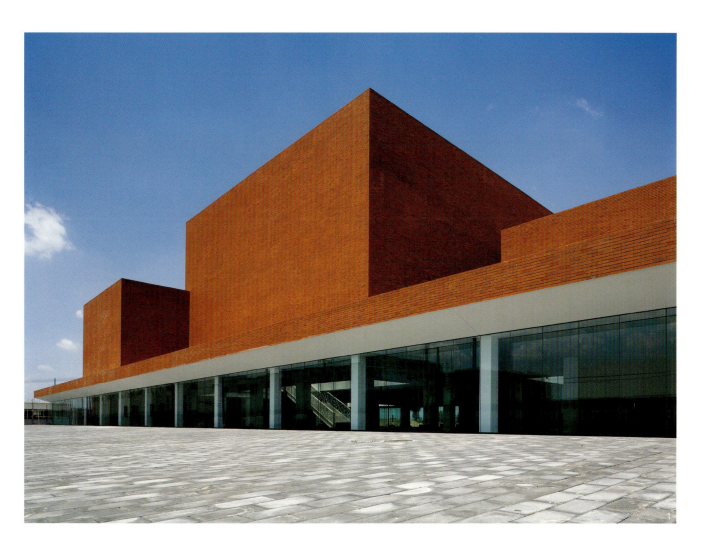

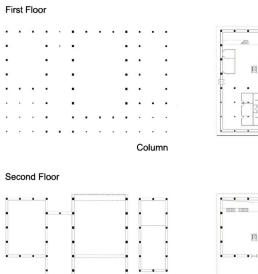

First Floor

Column

Second Floor

Column

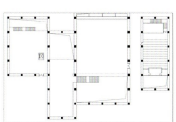

N

1	General view from south-east Außenansicht von Südosten
2	Floor plans Grundrisse

3 Courtyard Hof
4, 5 Ground floor interior views
Innenansichten Erdgeschoss

6, 9 Interior view exhibition hall
Innenansicht Ausstellungshalle
7 Exhibition hall, first floor
Ausstellungshalle, 1. Obergeschoss
8, 10 Sections Schnitte

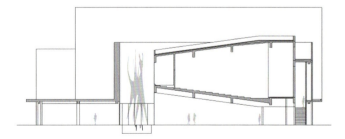

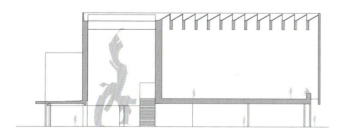

Jiakun Architects
2-7F, block11, 3# Yulin Nanlu
610041 Chengdu, Sichuan
Phone +86 28 85 56 88 99
Fax +86 28 85 58 94 91
jkads@263.net
www.jiakun.com

Jiakun Architects

LIU Jiakun

Established Gegründet
1999

Awards Preise

2007	Far East Award
2006	Architectural Record China Awards
2003	Chinese Architecture Art Prize
2003	Honor Prize of the 7th ARCASIA

Important Projects Wichtige Projekte

2008	Rebirth-brick Plan and Hu Huishan Memorial, Sichuan
2006	Times Rose Garden, landscape, and culture space design in Residential Community, Guangzhou
2006	The second period of Jindu
2006	Construction Exhibition Center, Qingpu
2006	Department of Sculpture of Sichuan Art Institute, Chongqing
2003–2004	Museum of Cultural Revolution Clocks, Anren, Sichuan
2001	Lu-ye-yuan Stone Sculpture Art Museum, Chengdu

10 Rebirth-brick Plan and HU Huishan Memorial, Sichuan

Location Standort: Wenchuan, Sichuan

Program Raumprogramm: Public architectural project Öffentliches Architekturprojekt

Architectural team Architektenteam: LIU Jiakun, CAI Kefei

Client Bauherr: Various Diverse

Design Entwurf: 2008

Construction Ausführung: 2008

Site area Fläche Baugrundstück: Increasing Wachsend

Gross building area Bruttogeschossfläche: N/A

Photographer Fotograf: Jiakun Architect & Associates

The rebirth-brick plan is a resource-manufacturing project to develop materials for the reconstruction of the 12 May 2008 Wenchuan earthquake-stricken zone. By using debris from the ruins as aggregates and pieces of wheat branch as reinforcing fiber and mixing them with cement, light-weight bricks can be made in the existing brick factories in the local area of the disaster zone. Apart from representing a physical "rebirth," it also represents a spiritual one, because even though homes have been destroyed, the remaining piles of debris still contain all the hopes and memories that once were. The rebirth-brick plan is also the most economical way to clean up the wreckage and to creatively use wheat branches often burned by farmers, causing air pollution. Some peasants in the earthquake-stricken zone have already moved into houses built using "rebirth bricks."

The memorial may be the smallest in the world; for HU Huishan, a fifteen-year-old girl, buried in the Wenchuan earthquake; her exact time of death remains unknown. She enjoyed literature and dreamed of becoming a writer. It is built in honor of all ordinary lives, reflecting an attitude of treasuring life. It is modeled on the pitched-roof makeshift tents frequently used in quake-stricken areas, with frame construction and rebirth bricks. Inside the memorial, the sidewalls display a few remembrances, which record HU Huishan's short life: photos, schoolbag, notebooks, deciduous tooth, umbilical cord … Her life did not leave much trace on society. The memorial is not solemn or loud; it is in memory of a flowery-aged maiden, displaying something of how a family in despair strives to live on.

Der Rebirth-brick-Plan ist eine Initiative zur Rückgewinnung von Bauressourcen zum Wiederaufbau der Region von Wenchuan, das am 12. Mai 2008 von einem verheerenden Erdbeben heimgesucht wurde. Durch die Verwendung von Schutt aus den Ruinen als Zuschlagstoff, Weizenhalmen als Faserverstärkung und Zement können in den noch vorhandenen Ziegeleien des Unglücksgebiets Leichtbauziegel hergestellt werden. Außer der physischen „Wiedergeburt" repräsentiert dies auch die spirituelle Auferstehung, denn trotz Zerstörung enthalten die Hausruinen doch all die Hoffnungen und Erinnerungen von einst. Der Rebirth-Brick-Plan stellt auch die ökonomischste Variante dar, die Zerstörungen zu beseitigen, und nutzt auf kreative Weise Weizenhalme, die oft von den Bauern verbrannt werden und Luftverschmutzung verursachen. Einige Bauern im Erdbebengebiet sind bereits in mit „Rebirth-Ziegeln" gebaute Häuser eingezogen.

Das Denkmal für HU Huishan, ein 15-jähriges Mädchen, das bei dem Beben verschüttet wurde, ist möglicherweise das kleinste der Welt. Ihr exakter Todeszeitpunkt ist unbekannt. Zu ihren Lebzeiten liebte sie die Literatur und träumte davon, Schriftstellerin zu werden. Das Denkmal ist den gewöhnlichen Menschen gewidmet und der Wertschätzung des Lebens im Allgemeinen. Es erinnert an die Form der spitzen Wanderzelte, die oft in Erdbebengebieten eingesetzt werden, und besteht aus einer Rahmenkonstruktion mit „Rebirth-Ziegeln". Im Inneren sind Erinnerungsstücke an HU Huishan ausgestellt: Fotos, eine Schultasche, Notizhefte, Milchzähne, Nabelschnur … Ihr Leben hinterließ keine großen Spuren. Das Denkmal ist nicht pathetisch oder laut – es ist nur das Andenken an ein junges Mädchen, das an den verzweifelten Versuch einer Familie erinnert, weiter zu leben.

1 HU Huishan Memorial, exterior view
  Außenansicht HU-Huishan-Mahnmal
2, 3 Rebirth-brick plan, production
  Rebirth-brick plan, Herstellung

11 Lu-ye-yuan Stone Sculpture Art Museum, Chengdu

Location Standort: **Chengdu, Sichuan**

Program Raumprogramm: **Museum**

Architectural team Architektenteam: **LIU Jiakun, WANG Lun**

Client Bauherr: **Private** Privat

Design Entwurf: **2001**

Construction Ausführung: **2001**

Gross building area Bruttogeschossfläche: **900 m²**

Photographer Fotograf: **Jiakun Architect & Associates**

This museum will display the carved antiques of Buddhism. Its architecture responds to the brief with "artificial stone-concrete" as a basic language. A unique tectonic method mixed with local construction standards give this building an experimental quality.

The architect wanted the museum to tell "an architectural story of man-made stone." To this end, he designed the building with a concrete frame and double walls made of an unusual combination of poured concrete and shale brick. Owing to the limitations of the local building trades in this part of Sichuan, the architect used the inner brick wall as a template, ensuring a vertical pour for the wall. Shale bricks also provided formwork to create a grid pattern on the concrete, which gives the walls texture and hides imperfections in the exposed material.

The architect uses the same rough concrete walls on the interior as he does on the exterior. He inserted clear glass in the intersections between the building's masonry volumes and carved out a large recess on the west façade for the entry ramp.

Visitors enter the museum from a ramp on the western side, over the small lotus pond to the second floor gallery. From here, they walk through an interior gallery space, which surrounds the open courtyard. Finally, walking down the stairs, they enter the gallery on the first floor.

Das Museum soll antike Skulpturen des Buddhismus zeigen. Die Architektur setzt die Bauaufgabe mit „künstlichem Betonstein" als Grundmotiv um. Seine einzigartige Bauweise, die örtliche Gepflogenheiten aufgreift, gibt diesem Bau eine experimentelle Note.

Der Architekt wollte, dass das Museum die „architektonische Geschichte von künstlichem Stein" erzählt. Zu diesem Zweck entwarf er das Gebäude als Betonkonstruktion mit zweischaligen Wänden aus der ungewöhnlichen Kombination von Ortbeton und Schieferziegeln. Da die technischen Möglichkeiten der Bauausführung in diesem Teil Sichuans begrenzt sind, wandte der Architekt eine innere Ziegelschale als Schablone an, um eine vertikale Ortbetonwand zu erreichen. Auch zur Schalung der Betonoberflächen wurden Schieferziegel verwendet, das entstandene Raster verleiht der Oberfläche Textur und kaschiert Mängel im Sichtbeton.

Der Architekt verwendet dieselben rohen Betonwände innen und außen. An den Schnittstellen der steinernen Baukörper setzte er Klarglas ein und schälte eine große Nische für die Eingangsrampe aus der Westfassade.

Besucher gelangen über diese Rampe und den kleinen Lotusteich zur Ausstellungshalle im zweiten Geschoss. Von dort durchschreiten sie die innen liegende Galerie um den Innenhof herum und gelangen letztlich über Treppen hinab zur Ausstellungshalle des ersten Geschosses.

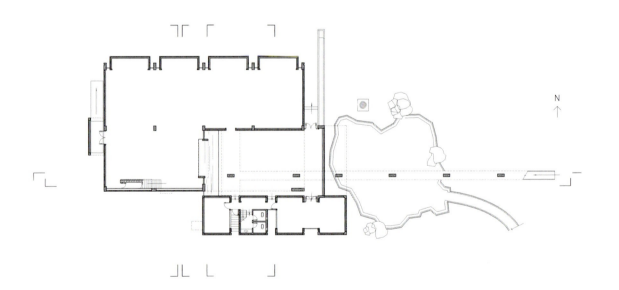

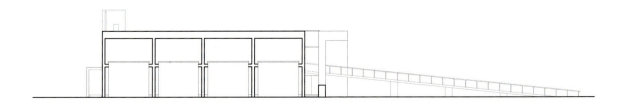

80   Jiakun Architects

1 Entrance bridge Eingangsbrücke
2 Exterior view from east
  Außenansicht von Osten
3 Ground floor plan
  Grundriss Erdgeschoss
4 Section Schnitt
5 Outdoor exhibition stage
  Ausstellungsbühne
6 Exit pond Wasseranlage

7	Entrance towards bridge
	Eingang Richtung Brücke
8	Section Schnitt
9	First floor plan
	Grundriss 1. Obergeschoss
10	Interior view Innenansicht

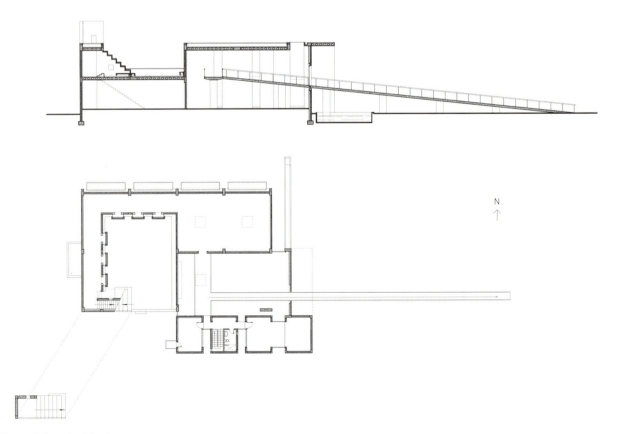

82   Jiakun Architects

12 Museum of Cultural Revolution Clocks, Sichuan

Location Standort: Anren Town, Dayi County, Sichuan

Program Raumprogramm: Museum

Architect Architekt: LIU Jiakun, WANG Lun

Client Bauherr: Sichuan Anren Cultural Industry Development Co., Ltd.

Design Entwurf: 2003–2004

Construction Ausführung: 2004

Site area Fläche Baugrundstück: 5,200 m²

Gross building area Bruttogeschossfläche: 3,885 m²

Photographer Fotograf: Jiakun Architects & Associates

This project was funded by a developer and collector and by a collection of private funds. The museum attracts people while the shops contribute to the running of the museum. Their co-existence demonstrates mutual support and successful interaction between business and culture. The museum is situated at the center of the site, leaving the surrounding area free for shops. As commercial zones have become very popular, the museum taps into the hustle and bustle of the surrounding commercial area while providing the tranquility of a museum area in sharp contrast to it. The gap between commercial reality and historical relics is reinforced, creating a unique sense of location. This structure is comparable to that of a temple of the traditional Chinese city, which also incorporated peripheral commerce and residence. From a design perspective, the shops along the streets have been allowed to develop according to business requirements. The commercial-residential area facing the street, known as "mundane space," is more or less loose, yet complex. In contrast, the clear bright brick of the museum and the typical classical patterns including round, square and crisscross applied to construct the "holy space," create a special singular, extreme, pure, and fanatical atmosphere.

Das Museum, begründet durch einen Projektentwickler und Sammler sowie private Förderer, ist ein Publikumsmagnet, während die integrierten Läden zur Finanzierung beitragen – ein gelungenes Beispiel für gegenseitige Unterstützung und das erfolgreiche Zusammenwirken von Wirtschaft und Kultur. Das Museum liegt in der Mitte des Grundstücks und lässt die übrige Fläche für die Geschäfte frei: Mitten im prallen Leben des Shoppingviertels bietet die Stille des Museumsbereichs einen unerwarteten Kontrast. Die Kluft zwischen kommerzieller Realität und historischen Reliquien wird betont und beschwört einen einzigartigen Genius Loci. Dieser Bau ist vergleichbar mit dem Tempel der traditionellen chinesischen Stadt, der ebenfalls Kommerz und Wohnen in seiner Umgebung integrierte. Aus entwurflicher Sicht wurden nur die Ansichten der Läden entlang der Straße vorgegeben, damit sie sich gemäß den kommerziellen Erfordernissen entwickeln konnten. Diese Mischung aus Kommerz und Wohnen, auch „alltäglicher Raum" genannt, ist mehr oder weniger lose und doch komplex. Im Kontrast dazu erzeugen das strenge, helle Mauerwerk des Museums und die typischen, klassischen Formen (wie Kreis, Quadrat und Zickzack), die für den „heiligen Kern" verwendet wurden, eine außergewöhnliche Atmosphäre mit extremer, nahezu „fanatischer" Wirkung.

1, 4	Exhibition hall Ausstellungshalle
2	Building site of the flag exhibition Fläche für die Flaggenausstellung
3	Site plan Lageplan

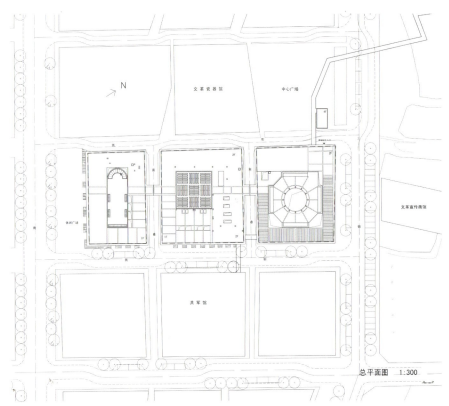

86 Jiakun Architects

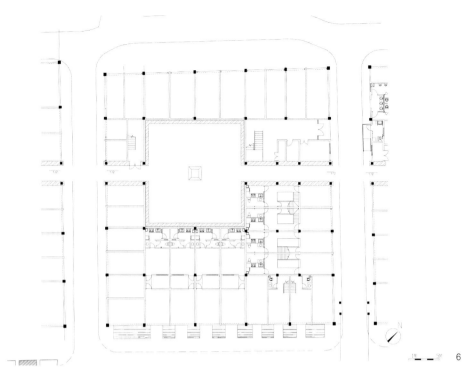

5 Courtyard inside the bell
  Hof in der Glocke
6 Part of ground floor plan
  Teil des Grundrisses, Erdgeschoss
7 Section Schnitt
8 Elevation Ansicht

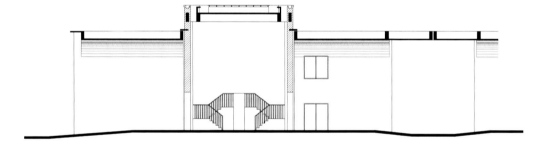

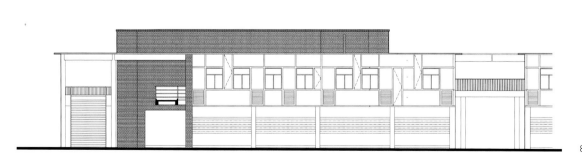

MADA s.p.a.m.
Architecture design office
No. 2, Lane 134, Xinle Road, Xuhui
District, Shanghai, China 200031
Phone + 86 21 5404 1166
Fax + 86 21 5404 6646
office@madaspam.com

MADA s.p.a.m.

MA Qingyun

Partners
CHEN Zhanhui
HUANG Rong

Associate Partners
YANG Yu
WANG Jianfeng
FUJIMORI Ryo

Established Gegründet
1999

Awards Preise

2008	Projects in Xi'an selected Top 10 projects of ICIP, Russia
2007	BIDV, Vietnam, Award of International Architecture Design
2006	Project of Ningbo Southern CBD won the first prize of International Architecture and Art Biennial in China
2005	selected in 10x10 by Phaidon Press, UK
2004	H.I.P., Beijing, MAPIC Best Design Award
2003	Chinese Architecture Art Prize

Important Projects Wichtige Projekte

2009	Xi' an Television and Broadcast Center, Xi' an
2008	Guanghualu SOHO, Beijing
2007	Jiangxi Natural History Museum, Jiangxi
2007	Jade Village, Xi'an
2007	Ningbo Liansheng International Plaza plot B, Ningbo
2006	Shanghai Greenland Chuansha, Shanghai

Guanghualu SOHO, Beijing

Location Standort: Chaoyang district, Beijing
Program Raumprogramm: Commercial, office Gewerbe, Büro
Project architect Architekt: MA Qingyun
Client Bauherr: SOHO China
Design Entwurf: MA Qingyun
Construction Ausführung: 2008
Site area Fläche Baugrundstück: 10,189 m²
Gross building area Bruttogeschossfläche: 75,438 m²
Photographer Fotograf: SOHO China, MADA s.p.a.m.

SOHO has become a name with tradition that will last into the future. However, is it a name stamp or name brand? During the proposal process, in our over-sensitivity to the name Soho, we attempted to extend its power by suggesting two design schemes named, SO-HILL and SO-ROCK. People generally choose to live and work on hills. In agrarian society, a hill is a symbol of intelligence and nobility; it has become a prime address postfix within the contemporary city. The rock is a Chinese symbol of endurance and persistence; it has become an instrument of civilization and advancement.

This hill-like building consists of three parts. The lowest part is for retail; it is the fullest, providing maximum usable retail areas and is lit from the "caves" in the middle section. The second and middle part provides office space for small companies, offering a great sense of community. Voids and folds form spaces for communal facilities such as lounges, gardens, and conference rooms. The third area, located at the top of the hill, (Rock) consists of two clustered penthouses for large companies, giving them a sense of prestige and seclusion.

Mit dem Namen des chinesischen Immobilienentwicklers SOHO verbinden sich gleichermaßen Tradition wie Zukunft. Kann ein solcher Name schon als Marke gelten? In Reaktion auf die Kraft des Namens schlugen die Designer in der Konzeptionsphase vor, ihre Wirkung zu erweitern und entwarfen „SO-HILL" (SO-Hügel) und „SO-ROCK" (SO-Fels).
Die Grundidee: Die Menschen neigen generell dazu, auf Hügeln zu leben und zu arbeiten. In der bäuerlichen Gesellschaft Symbol für Intelligenz und Erhabenheit, haben sich die Höhenlagen zur „ersten Adresse" innerhalb der modernen Stadt entwickelt. Der Fels hingegen ist ein chinesisches Symbol für Ausdauer und Beständigkeit und ist zu einem Instrument für Zivilisation und Fortschritt geworden.

Der hügelartige Baukörper SO-HILL besteht aus drei Teilen. Der unterste dient dem Einzelhandel: Er ist der geräumigste, bietet maximale Verkaufsnutzfläche und wird von den „Höhlen" im Mittelteil beleuchtet. Der zweite, mittlere Teil bietet kleinen Firmen Büroflächen und schafft eine angenehme Arbeitsatmosphäre. Lufträume und Nischen bilden Raum für Sitzbereiche, Gärten und Versammlungen. Der dritte Bereich auf der Hügelkuppe (SO-ROCK) besteht aus zwei Penthäusern, die großen Firmen in abgeschiedener und prestigereicher Umgebung Platz bieten.

1, 2 Exterior views along Guanghua Road
Außenansichten an der Gunghua Road
3 North elevation Nordansicht
4 Interior view Innenansicht
5 Ground floor plan
Grundriss Erdgeschoss

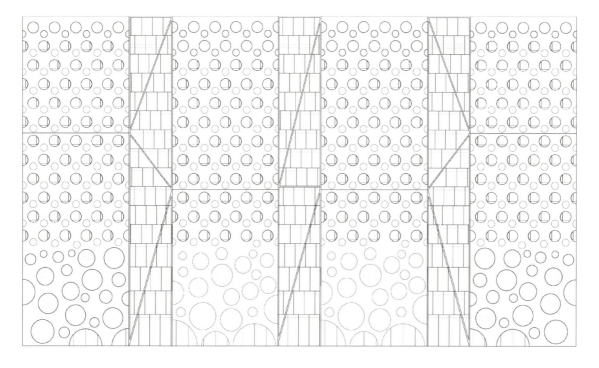

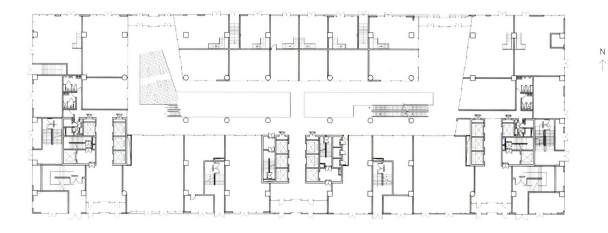

14 Xi'an Television and Broadcast Center, Xi'an

Location Standort: Xi'an, Shaanxi

Program Raumprogramm: Office, media, commercial Büros, Medien- und Geschäftsnutzung

Project architect Architekt: MA Qingyun

Client Bauherr: Xi'an Broadcast and Television Bureau

Design Entwurf: MA Qingyun

Construction Ausführung: 2009

Site area Fläche Baugrundstück: 62,854 m²

Gross building area Bruttogeschossfläche: 81,117 m²

Photographer Fotograf: MADA s.p.a.m.

This project has inherited the generosity as well as the concise and stately characteristics of the Hang Tang culture of Xi'an; an integrated whole enhances the perception of scale within the larger context of the site. Various programs are enclosed by a symbolic "wall," which both compensates for height differences in the surrounding site and makes reference to the land art element of a Xi'an Wall; it is also a metaphor for Xi'an TV as a "Media City."

The site forms an extension of the typology and landscape of the imitated Tang Dynasty Park of Qu; it reflects traditional Hang Tang large-scale construction, adhering to axial organization. The architectural axis is aligned to the Qu Jiang Axis to the north, extending the existing north-south axis of Qu Jiang Park and emphasizing major differences in height within the site, which descends from north to west. This shift in height has also been integrated into the interior of the building to both incorporate the natural landscape of Qu Jiang and to highlight the monumentality of this grand public space.

Prägnanz, Würde und Großzügigkeit gelten als charakteristische Merkmale der historischen Hang-Tang-Kultur von Xi'an, die dieses Projekt widerspiegeln soll. Der Entwurf ist durch ein Gesamtkonzept geprägt, das es ermöglichen soll, die unterschiedliche Maßstäblichkeit im größeren, örtlichen Kontext wahrzunehmen. Eine symbolische „Mauer" verbindet die unterschiedlichen Bereiche des Raumprogramms – in Anlehnung an den skulpturalen Charakter typischer Xi'an-Mauern. Sie dient zudem dazu, Höhenunterschiede auszugleichen und Xi'an TV als „Medienstadt" zu kennzeichnen.

Das Grundstück erweitert die Typologie und Landschaft des imitierten Tang-Dynastie-Parks von Qu. Wie traditionelle Hang-Tang-Großbauten folgt es einer axialen Organisation: Die architektonische Achse ist auf die Qu-Jiang-Achse im Norden ausgerichtet, erweitert die bestehende Nord-Süd-Achse des Qu-Jiang-Parks und betont die Höhenunterschiede innerhalb des Grundstücks, das von Norden nach Westen deutlich abfällt. Der Höhenwechsel ist auch ins Innere des Gebäudes eingeflossen, um die Landschaft von Qu Jiang einzubeziehen, aber auch um die Monumentalität dieses großartigen öffentlichen Platzes hervorzuheben.

1 Exterior view Außenansicht
2 Ground floor plan
  Grundriss Erdgeschoss

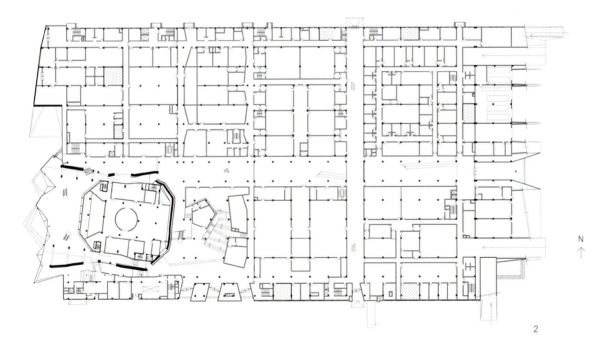

3 Exterior view from the south
  Außenansicht von Süden
4 South elevation Südansicht
5 Longitudinal section Längsschnitt
6, 7 Details of south wall
  Details der Südwand

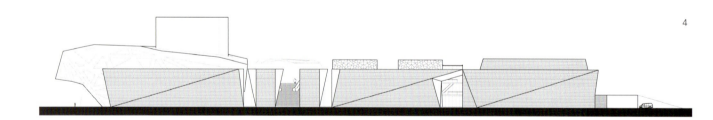

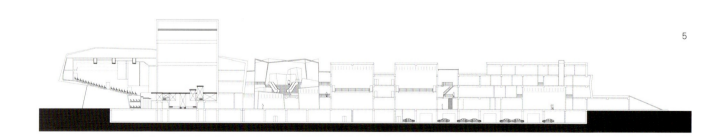

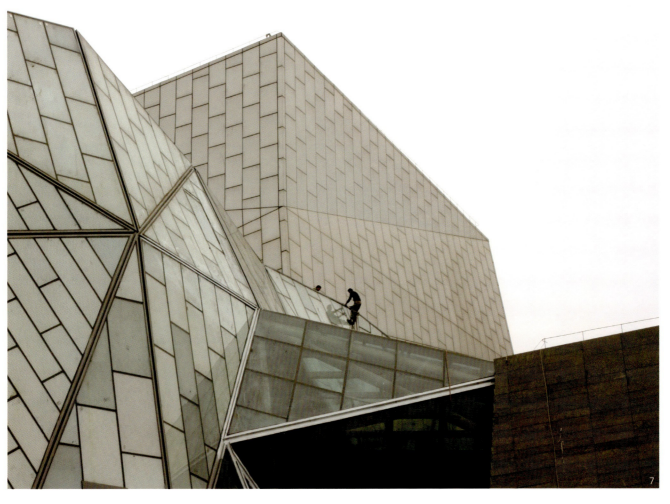

Jade Village (Well Hall, Father's House, Wine Dorm), Xi'an

Location Standort: Xi'an, Shaanxi

Program Raumprogramm: Hotel, mixed use Hotel, Mischnutzung

Architectural team Architektenteam: MA Qingyun

Client Bauherr: Private Privat

Construction Ausführung: 2007

Site area Fläche Baugrundstück: 13,654 m²

Gross building area Bruttogeschossfläche: 19,201 m²

Photographer Fotograf: MADA s.p.a.m.

This site is located in Jade Mountain County; it sits on the highland between a riverbed to the south and a mountain range to the north. Although it is situated at a comfortable distance from the village, it is not too detached, boasting a great location and spectacular views of the surrounding mountains and fields. It is within walking distance of Jade Valley winery and vineyard. A small private museum and a traditional courtyard home have also been constructed within the general area.

As wine-making and the passion that goes with it spread, a new economy had to be established to incorporate wine, architecture, and tourism. Well Hall was proposed as a hotel first to be turned into a wine resort in future. This was the first time for a building of such height to be proposed and the second time for a project to be built using entirely local labor and craftsman. At first the local builders did not have knowledge of building masonry walls; however they were able to learn from an external designer. As the local style is single-story, they had never before built a two-story structure.

The design of the house MA Qingyun built for his father is playing on the contrast of river and mountains, of smooth and rough textures. The use of concrete is reduced to a minimum, it forms a frame for the local materials stone and wood. This collision of rough, organic materials with a highly regulated, spare form gives the house a very special quality.

The Wine Dorm is an existing office building turned into a hotel, which is perfectly integrated into the natural surroundings.

Im Hochland des Jade-Mountain-Bezirks zwischen einem Fluss im Süden und einer Bergkette im Norden gelegen, zeichnet sich dieses Grundstück durch spektakuläre Aussichten über die umgebenden Berge und Flüsse aus. Es liegt in komfortabler Entfernung zum nächsten Dorf, ist aber keineswegs abgelegen: Das Jade-Valley-Weingut mit seiner Weinkellerei ist zu Fuß erreichbar, ein privates Museum und ein traditionelles Hofwohnhaus, beide neu errichtet, befinden sich in der Nähe.

Mit der wachsenden Verbreitung und Bedeutung des Weinanbaus ist es erforderlich geworden, die Verbindung von Wein, Architektur und Tourismus neu zu artikulieren. Well Hall ist das erste Hotel in dieser Gegend, das in Zukunft zu einem Wein-Resort entwickelt werden soll. Erstmalig wurde ein Bauwerk hier vorgeschlagen. Es war das zweite Mal, dass ein Bau gänzlich durch lokale Arbeiter und Handwerker realisiert wurde. Erstmalig haben örtliche Kräfte von auswärtigen Architekten das Mauern erlernt, erstmalig bauten sie auch ein zweigeschossiges Haus innerhalb einer regionalen eingeschossigen Typologie.

Das Haus, das MA Qingyun hier für seinen Vater baute, spielt mit dem Gegensatz von Fluss und Berg, glatten und rauen Oberflächen. Die Verwendung von Beton ist auf ein Minimum reduziert, als Rahmen für die lokalen Materialien Stein und Holz. Das Zusammentreffen von rohen, organischen Materialien und hochorganisierter, disziplinierter Form verleiht dem Haus eine ganz besondere Qualität.

Das Wine Dorm ist ein ehemaliges Bürogebäude, das zu einem Hotel umgebaut wurde und sich perfekt in die umgebende Landschaft einfügt.

1 View of Jade Village
Blick auf Jade Village
2 Jade valley site map
Lageplan Jade Valley

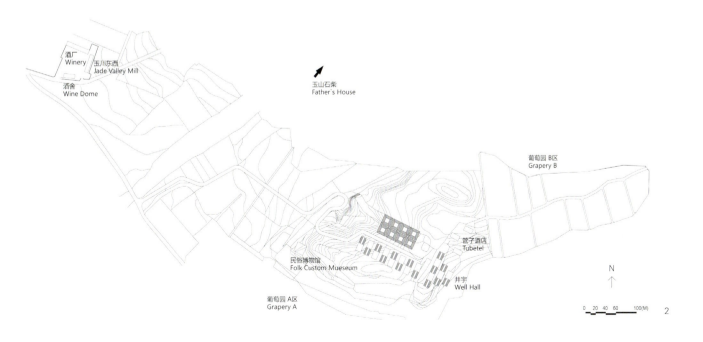

101

3 Exterior view of Well Hall Hotel
Ansicht Well Hall Hotel
4,5 Interior views of Well Hall Hotel
Innenansichten von Well Hall Hotel

6 Exterior views of Father's House
Außenansichten von Father's House
7,8 Interior views of Father's House
Innenansichten von Father's House

7

8

9 Exterior view of Wine Dorm
  Außenansicht von Wine Dorm
10 Wine Dorm, view from north
  Wine Dorm, Nordansicht
11 Interior view of Wine Dorm
  Wine Dorm, Innenansicht

standardarchitecture
268 Chengfu Road, Room 203 Building
#4, Haidian District 100080 Beijing
Phone +86 10 6263 4351
Fax +86 10 6263 0248
pro-sa@263.net
www.standardarchitecture.cn

standardarchitecture

ZHANG Ke
ZHANG Hong
HOU Zhenghua
Claudia Taborda

Established Gegründet
2001

Awards Preise

2008	Young Architects Award of China Architectural Media Award (CAMA)
2006	WA Award (Winner), World Architecture Magazine

Important Projects Wichtige Projekte

2008	Namchabawa Visitor Centre, Tibet
2008	Yaluntzangpu Boat Terminal, Linzhi, Tibet
2008	Suzhou "An" Club Tea House, Suzhou
2008	Namchabawa Mulberry Tree Contemplation, Linzhi, Tibet
2007	Qingcheng Mountain Stone Courtyard Teahouse, Chengdu
2005	French Chinese Art Centre, Wuhan
2005	Yangshuo Storefronts, Guilin
2003	Beijing Dongbianmen Ming Dynasty Relics Park

16 Qingcheng Mountain Stone Courtyard, Chengdu

Location Standort: Chengdu, Sichuan

Program Raumprogramm: Commercial Geschäftliche Nutzung

Client Bauherr: Sichuan Jinlian Corporation

Design Entwurf: 2005–2006

Construction Ausführung: 2006–2007

Site area Fläche Baugrundstück: 600 m²

Gross building area Bruttogeschossfläche: 480 m²

Photographer Fotograf: CHEN Su

The "Stone Courtyard" tea house is located close to Daguan Town at the foot of Qingcheng Mountain near Chengdu. With a total area of 500 square meters, the tea house is actually comprised of five separate close-standing courtyard buildings. The first building is an empty front courtyard and the last building is residential, while the other three buildings function as tea courtyards.

Local craftsmen were involved in the design and construction of the wooden roof structure. From the interior, the wooden roof would be completely traditional if the columns near the patio had not been carefully removed.

The stone wall is built exclusively of a type of local slate, which will be covered in green moss in a few years after being exposed to the rainy, humid weather of Chengdu.

Das Teehaus „Stone Courtyard" liegt in der Nähe von Daguan am Fuße des Berges Qingcheng bei Chengdu. Bei einer Gesamtfläche von 500 Quadratmetern besteht das Teehaus eigentlich aus fünf dicht beieinander stehenden Hofgebäuden. Das erste Gebäude ist dabei ein umbauter Hof, das letzte ein Wohnhof und die dazwischen liegenden drei Gebäude fungieren als Teehöfe.

Örtliche Handwerker wurden für den Entwurf und die Konstruktion der hölzernen Dachkonstruktion herangezogen. Das Holzdach über dem Inneren wäre ein ganz traditionelles, wenn nicht die üblichen Hofstützen sorgsam entfernt worden wären.

Die Mauerwände bestehen durchweg aus lokalem Schiefer, der in ein paar Jahren durch das regnerische und feuchte Wetter Chengdus von grünem Moos überzogen sein wird.

1, 3	Interior details Innenansichten
2	Interior view of roof Innenansicht des Dachs
4	Exterior view Außenansicht

17 Suzhou "AN" Club Tea House, Suzhou

Location Standort: Suzhou, Jiangsu

Client Bauherr: Vanke Group

Design Entwurf: 2006–2007

Construction Ausführung: 2007–2008

Site area Fläche Baugrundstück: 4,500 m^2

Gross building area Bruttogeschossfläche: 3,700 m^2

Photographer Fotograf: CHEN Su

The Suzhou "AN" clubhouse building is formed by one single 500-meter-long, nine-meter-high wall, which folds many times to enclose numerous courtyards; this building starts from the betrayal of the doctrines of traditional Suzhou garden layouts.

The club has been shaped by a 500-meter-long folding wall, which also encloses thirteen separate courtyards. A delicate ribbon pierces the building, guiding people to enjoy the experience of "a different view with every step" within the spaces and landscapes. Each span has an irregular shape; different spans combine to form a kind of introverted space. Transverse bridges cut the spans into spaces with different functions, such as interiors, courtyards, atriums, water, and bridges, reinterpreting Suzhou tradition in a novel way.

Das „AN" Klubhaus in Suzhou wird von einer einzigen, 500 Meter langen und neun Meter hohen Wand gebildet, die sich mehrfach faltet und dabei eine Vielzahl von Höfen einschließt. Damit bricht es mit der Doktrin traditioneller Gartenarchitektur in Suzhou.

Insgesamt werden 13 verschiedene Höfe von der Wand eingeschlossen. Ein filigranes Band durchzieht das Gebäude und lässt die Besucher mit jedem Schritt eine neue Aussicht auf Landschaft und Raum genießen. Alle Abschnitte sind unterschiedlich geformt; verschiedene Abschnitte fügen sich zu einer Art introvertiertem Raum. Querverlaufende Brücken unterteilen die Abschnitte in Bereiche mit unterschiedlicher Funktion, wie zum Beispiel Innenräume, Höfe, Atrien, Wasser und Brücken – und interpretieren die Suzhou-Tradition auf neue Weise.

1 Exterior view of 500-meter-wall
  Außenansicht der 500 Meter langen Mauer
2 Site plan Lageplan

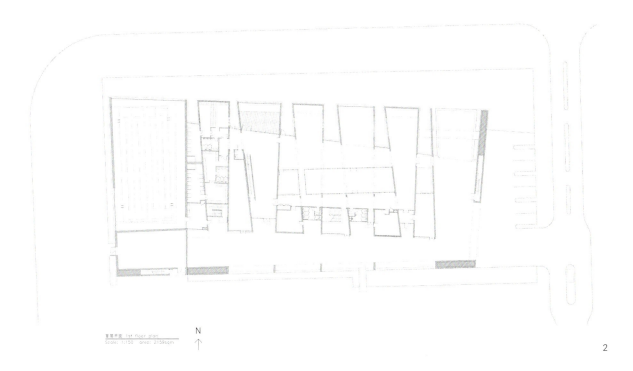

3, 4, 5 Exterior details
Außenansichten
6, 7 Sections Schnitte

8 Pond Teich
9, 12 Exterior details Außenansichten
10, 11 Elevations Ansichten

18 Yaluntzangpu Boat Terminal, Linzhi, Tibet

Location Standort: Linzhi, Tibet

Program Raumprogramm: Public boat terminal Öffentliche Bootsanlegestelle

Collaborating design institution In Zusammenarbeit mit: China Academy of Building Research Architectural Design Institute & Tibet Youdao Architecture Associates

Client Bauherr: Tibet Tourism Co., Ltd

Design Entwurf: 2007

Construction Ausführung: 2008

Site area Fläche Baugrundstück: 1,000 m²

Gross building area Bruttogeschossfläche: 430 m²

Photographer Fotograf: CHEN Su

This small boat terminal is located near the little village of Pai Town in the Linzhi area of Tibet Autonomous Region. As the remotest stop along the Yaluntzangpu River, it allows both local people and travelers from outside to journey by water deep into the valley, taking them to the foot of Namchabawa Snow Mountain.

With a total area of only 430 square meters, the building program is quite basic. It includes a waiting lounge, a ticket office, a few toilets and a room in which people can stay overnight should the weather become too fierce to travel on the river. The building is defined by a series of ramps that rise from the water to wind around several large poplar trees, ending up suspended over the water. From a distance, the building appears to be completely merged with the riverbank topography, becoming part of the greater landscape.

The construction materials used are mainly local. All of the walls and roofs are made of nearby rock. The walls were built by Tibetan masonry builders in their traditional patterns. Window and door frames, ceilings and floors are all made of local timber.

Von dieser Bootsanlegestelle in der Nähe des kleinen Dorfes Pai im Bezirk Linzhi, Tibet, dem letzten Außenposten entlang des Yaluntzangpu, bringt der Fluss Einheimische und auswärtige Reisende tiefer in das Tal, bis zum Fuß des Namchabawa Snow Mountain.

Mit einer Gesamtfläche von nur 430 Quadratmetern ist das Raumprogramm recht einfach: ein Warteraum, ein Fahrkartenschalter, Toiletten und ein Raum, in dem Passagiere übernachten können, falls das Wetter einmal eine Weiterreise auf dem Fluss verhindern sollte. Das Gebäude wird von Rampen gebildet, die vom Wasser aufsteigen, sich um einige große Pappeln winden und schließlich über das Wasser auskragen. Aus der Entfernung scheint das Gebäude vollkommen in der Ufertopografie aufzugehen und fügt sich nahtlos in das Landschaftspanorama ein.

Es wurden hauptsächlich lokale Baumaterialien verwendet. Alle Wände und Decken bestehen aus lokalem Felsgestein. Die Wände wurden von tibetischen Maurern in traditionellem Verband errichtet. Fenster- und Türrahmen, Decken und Fußböden bestehen allesamt aus örtlichem Holz.

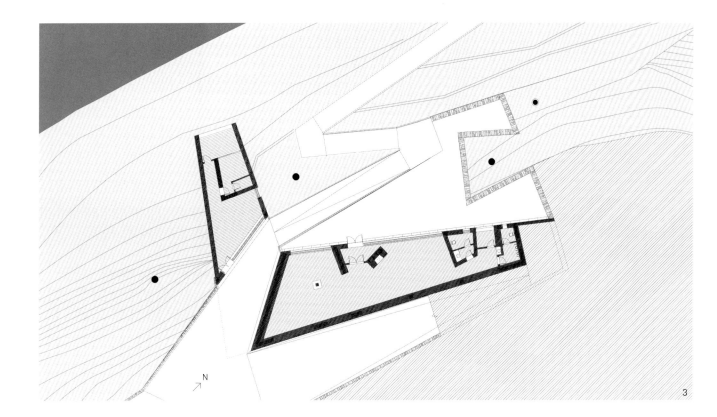

1 Entrance from south
  Eingang von Süden
2 Interior courtyard to river from south
  Innenhof zum Fluss von Süden
3 Ground floor plan
  Grundriss Erdgeschoss
4 Sectional elevation east-west
  Schnittansicht Ost-West
5 View from river Ansicht vom Fluss
6 Ramp to roof Rampe auf das Dach

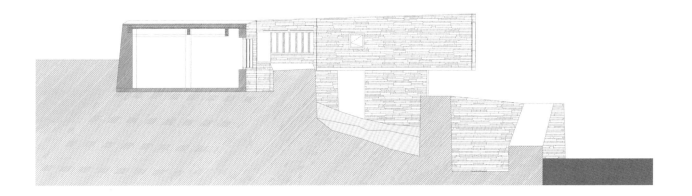

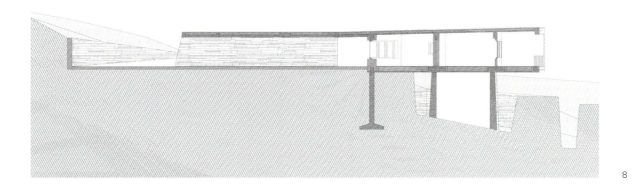

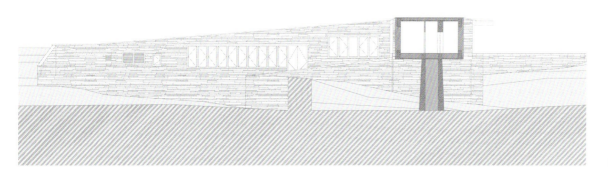

124 standardarchitecture

7	Passageway Durchgang
8	Section through shelter Schnitt durch Ruheraum
9	Sectional elevation Schnittansicht
10	Interior view of shelter Innenansicht Ruheraum

Studio Pei-Zhu
B-413 Tiantai Business Center No. 107 N.
Dongsi Street 100007, Beijing
Phone +86 10 64 01 66 57
Fax +86 10 64 03 89 67
office@studiozp.com
www.studiopeizhu.com

Studio Pei-Zhu

Awards Preise

2008	DFA Grand Award
2008	DFA Special Award for Culture
2008	Perspective Award, Best Architectural Project
2007	Design Vanguard, *Architectural Record,* New York
2006	China Award, *Architectural Record,* New York
2004	WA China Architectural Prize
2004	Digital Beijing, an Olympic project for 2008, Beijing, won the first prize in national design competition

Important Projects Wichtige Projekte

2008	Publishing House, Beijing
2007	Guggenheim Museum, Beijing
2007	Guggenheim Art Pavilion, Abu Dhabi
2007	CAI Guoqiang Courtyard House Renovation, Beijing
2007	Art Museum for artist YUE Minjun
2006	Blur Hotel, Beijing

ZHU Pei
WU Tong

Established Gegründet
2005

19 CAI Guoqiang Courtyard House Renovation, Beijing

Location Standort: Beijing

Program Raumprogramm: Art studio and residence Künstleratelier, Wohnen

Client Bauherr: CAI Guoqiang

Design Entwurf: 2006–2007

Construction Ausführung: 2007

Site area Fläche Baugrundstück: 910.33 m²

Gross building area Bruttogeschossfläche: 413 m²

Photographer Fotograf: FANG Zhenning

This project calls for the restoration of a historically significant classical Chinese *siheyuan* courtyard house, and a new building addition within its compounds. The main challenge is that it is situated very close to the Forbidden City; the addition therefore had to be sensitive to its external surroundings, *hutong* neighborhood, and internal courtyard configuration. The attitude developed for this project was one of sensitive regeneration, in which contemporary and modern buildings can symbiotically co-exist with traditional structures. Old architecture was well respected and preserved by traditional materials, construction technologies, local skilled craftsmen and builders. The new addition has a metal facade of titanium-aluminum alloy, glass and steel. It expresses a futuristic notion while also taking advantage of its reflective properties to pay homage to the old.

The double courtyard configuration was restored into its intended void, giving presence to the south-facing buildings. The three building parts that form the two courtyards were given three spatial themes. The north part was defined as a "three-dimensional installation." The old wooden structure of this space was exposed to express its strength and power. The middle section was defined as "two-dimensional Chinese painting"—white walls dominate the interior, expressing a sense of relaxation and grace. The southern area was defined as "futuristic space." The new "invisible" building, however, was created as an object that floats in the larger southern courtyard to face the traditional structures. It is detailed to be independent from the existing courtyard walls to cause as little impact as possible on the old structure; visually and physically light.

Dieses Projekt umfasst den Wiederaufbau eines historisch bedeutenden, klassischen chinesischen Siheyuan-Hofhauses und einen neuen Erweiterungsbau. Die größte Herausforderung war die Nähe des Ensembles zur Verbotenen Stadt: Die Erweiterung musste sensibel zwischen der äußeren Umgebung aus Hutongs – traditioneller einstöckiger Bebauung – sowie dem Hofensemble vermitteln. Daraus entwickelte sich eine Haltung des behutsamen Wiederaufbaus, ein symbiotisches Miteinander von zeitgenössischer moderner und traditioneller Architektur. Die alte Architektur wurde mittels traditioneller Materialien und Bautechniken und mithilfe von lokalen Handwerkern und Bauarbeitern restauriert. Dem Anbau verleiht eine Metallfassade aus einer Titan-Aluminiumlegierung, Glas und Stahl eine futuristische Anmutung, gleichzeitig spiegelt sich in dieser Hülle der Altbau – das Neue erweist durch Spiegelung dem Alten die Ehre.

Das Doppelhofschema wurde in seiner ursprünglichen, leeren Form wieder hergestellt, was den nach Süden orientierten Gebäuden zu neuer Geltung verhilft. Die drei Gebäudeteile, welche die beiden Höfe bilden, wurden räumlich thematisiert. Im nördlichen Teil wurde die alte Holzstruktur freigelegt, eine kraftvolle „dreidimensionale Installation". Der Mittelteil wurde zum „zweidimensionalen chinesischen Gemälde" erklärt: Weiße Wände dominieren das Innere und strahlen Ruhe und Eleganz aus. Der südliche Bereich wurde zum „futuristischen Raum". Das neue „unsichtbare" Gebäude war dabei als Objekt gedacht, das im größeren südlichen Hof schwebt, gegenüber den traditionellen Gebäudeteilen. Von den bestehenden Hofaußenwänden losgelöst, um den Eingriff in die alte Baustruktur möglichst zu minimieren, strahlt es visuelle wie physische Leichtigkeit aus.

1 South courtyard after renovation
Südlicher Innenhof nach Renovierung
2 Site plan Lageplan

130 Studio Pei-Zhu

3 Eastern entranceway
  Östlicher Eingangsweg
4 Longitudinal section Längsschnitt
5 Rendering bird's eye view
  Rendering Vogelperspektive
6, 7 Interior walls Innenwände

20 Blur Hotel, Beijing

Location Standort: Beijing

Program Raumprogramm: Business hotel and cultural facility Businesshotel, Kultur

Client Bauherr: China Resource

Design Entwurf: 2004–2005

Construction Ausführung: 2005–2006

Gross building area Bruttogeschossfläche: 10,176 m²

Photographer Fotograf: FANG Zhenning, SHU He

This structure was a governmental office building in the 1990s, built to replace typical local architecture, siheyuan, ignoring the rhythm and consistency of the old Beijing city center. It disrupted the once free-flowing and hierarchical city plan. Like a "tumor" within the ancient Ming dynasty core, it has resulted in the creation of a disjointed and incomprehensible city center. In response to this problem, the project, located on the site of a large government office beside the western Gate of the Forbidden City, is an experimental "urban acupuncture." Rather than operating to remove the tumor (in other words demolish yet again), a far less disruptive and harmful method is to leave it in place and simply neutralize its ill effects. As a refurbishment proposal, the project aims to harmonize the existing building with its surroundings without resorting to backward looking pastiche, thus providing a beacon for the renewal of the surrounding area.

The first strategy employed with this end in mind was to open up the ground floor of the building to create a layer of traversable space occupied by public-oriented programs. The next approach aims to integrate the building more with the local building typology of the siheyuan, or courtyard house. By simply carving into the concrete slab floors of the existing building, an arrangement of alternating vertical courtyards has been created, replicating the spatial arrangement of the surrounding hutongs. The third and final tactic deals with the exterior of the building, wrapping it in a continuous and semi-transparent façade. In reference to local tradition, this skin is based on the image of a Chinese lantern. Allowing light out and into the building on every floor, it diffuses the building into a single yet permeable object.

In den Neunzigern als staatliches Bürogebäude errichtet, sollte dieser Bau die typische lokale Wohnhofarchitektur der Siheyuan verdrängen. Der städtebauliche Rhythmus und Zusammenhang des alten Zentrums von Peking wurden ignoriert, der einst frei fließende, hierarchische Stadtgrundriss durchbrochen. Wie ein Tumor im alten Stadtkern der Mingdynastie zerriss das Gebäude das Stadtzentrum. Das Projekt auf dem Grundstück eines staatlichen Bürobaus neben dem Westtor der Verbotenen Stadt versucht als Reaktion auf dieses Problem eine Art experimenteller „städtebaulicher Akupunktur". Anstatt den „Tumor" zu entfernen (was erneute Zerstörung bedeutet hätte), wurde es als weit weniger brutal und schädlich empfunden, ihn an seinem Ort zu belassen und seine Symptome einfach zu neutralisieren. Als Sanierungsvorschlag versucht das Projekt, ohne nostalgisch zu werden, das bestehende Gebäude mit seiner Umgebung in Einklang zu bringen – als leuchtendes Beispiel für den Stadtumbau in dieser Gegend.

Die erste Strategie zur Erreichung dieses Ziels war die Öffnung des Erdgeschosses, um eine frei zugängliche Ebene mit einem öffentlichen Raumprogramm zu schaffen. Der zweite Schritt sollte das Gebäude stärker in den Kontext der typischen Hofhäuser integrieren. Durch einfaches Durchschneiden der Betongeschossplatten des Bestandsbaus wurde eine vertikale Anordnung verschiedener Höfe erreicht, die an das räumliche Gefüge der umgebenden Hutongs erinnert. Der dritte und letzte taktische Zug: Das Äußere des Baus wurde mit einer durchgängigen, transluzenten Fassade verkleidet. In Anlehnung an die lokale Tradition erinnert die Hülle an eine chinesische Laterne: Sie lässt auf jeder Ebene Licht hinein und hinaus und verwandelt das Gebäude zu einem einzigen, durchlässigen Objekt.

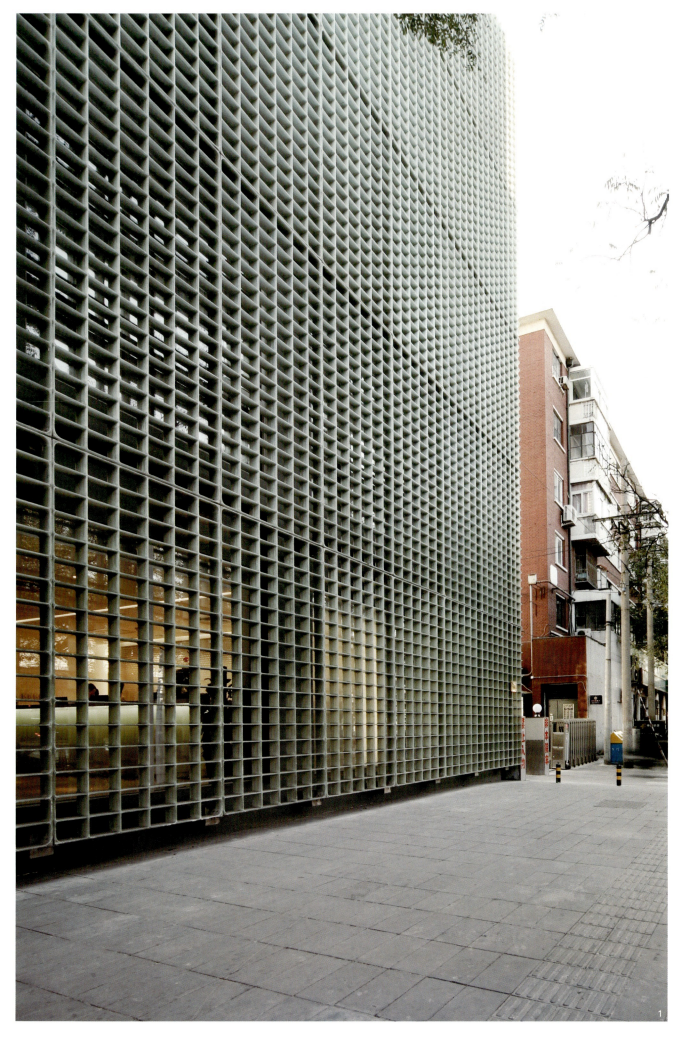

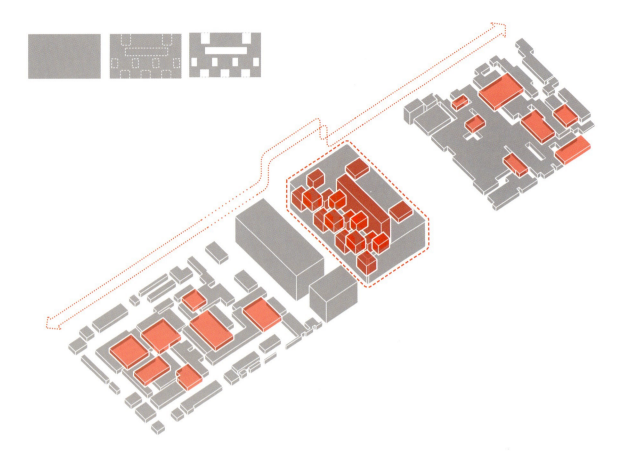

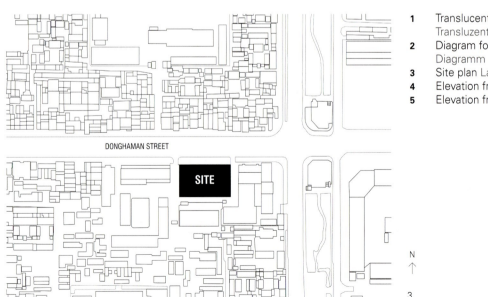

1 Translucent façade screen
　Transluzente Schicht der Außenfassade
2 Diagram for vertical courtyards
　Diagramm der vertikalen Höfe
3 Site plan Lageplan
4 Elevation from the north Nordansicht
5 Elevation from the west Westansicht

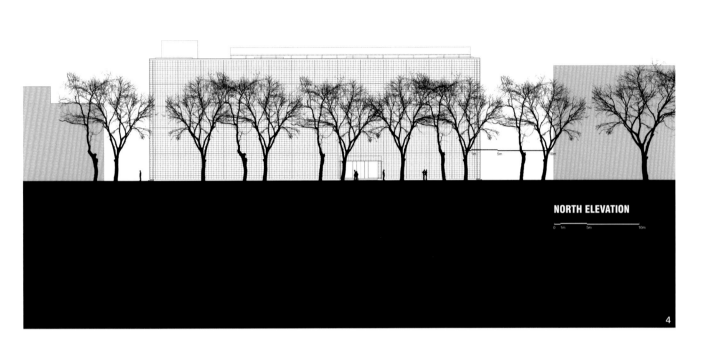

NORTH ELEVATION

4

WEST ELEVATION

5

6	Typical courtyard
	Typischer Innenhof
7	Façade screen Fassadenschicht
8	Model Modell
9	Longitudinal section Längsschnitt
10	Cross section Querschnitt

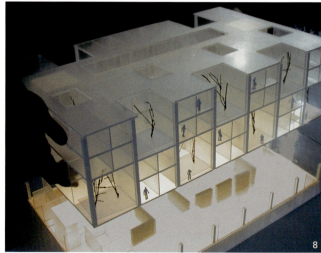

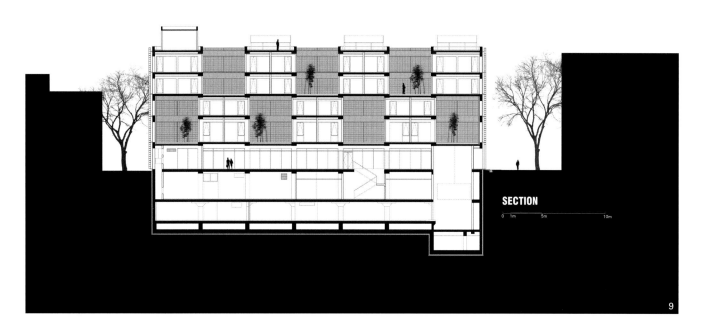

SECTION
0 1m   5m   10m

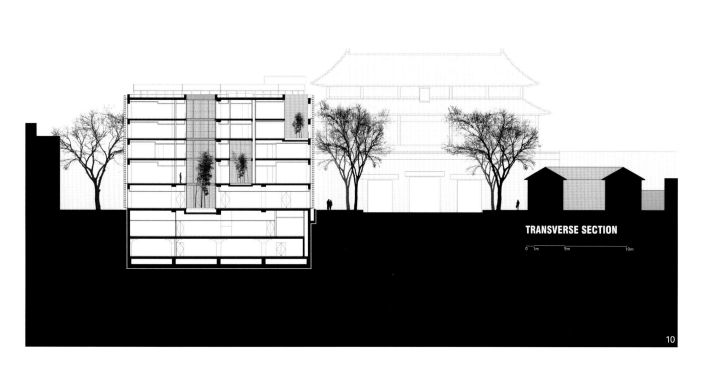

TRANSVERSE SECTION
0 1m   5m   10m

21 Publishing House, Beijing

Location Standort: Beijing

Program Raumprogramm: Creativity center for the publishing industry Kreatives Zentrum für das Verlagswesen

Client Bauherr: Beijing Publishing Group

Design Entwurf: 2006–2007

Construction Ausführung: 2007–2008

Gross building area Bruttogeschossfläche: 10,980 m²

Photographer Fotograf: LIU Ruohan, LI Yongquan

This project is the result of the renovation of an existing twelve-story office building of Beijing Publishing Corporation. It aims to be a center that promotes creativity within the publishing industry and that increases public interest in publishing. The site has a prominent corner location on Beijing's busy north third ring road, on the north-south axis running between the Forbidden City in the center and the Olympic Park in the North.

Working from this premise, the project seeks to create a microcosm of the surrounding urban fabric within one building—a MicroCity focused on publishing. The existing homogenous, compartmentalized office building was transformed into a heterogeneous mix of linked spaces for work, learning, retail, and leisure. Public and communal space has been introduced into a closed building; vertical paths of communication between floors opened up and outdoor spaces connecting the occupants with the city were created.

A series of cantilevers of varying size have thus been constructed, extending the existing floors. The changes are concentrated on the north and west sides, allowing links to be formed between floors with only minimal modification of the existing reinforced concrete structure, and also creating external terraces. Circulation and communal areas are located in these newly created spaces, which rise from the ground floor to the roof, forming a giant window to life and movement inside the building from the congested six-lane ring road.

Mit der Sanierung soll das zwölfstöckige Bürogebäude der Beijing Publishing Corporation zu einem kreativen Zentrum des Verlagswesens werden und das öffentliche Interesse an der Branche steigern. Das Grundstück liegt an einer markanten Ecke an Pekings geschäftiger Dritter Nördlicher Ringstraße an der Nord-Südachse, die zwischen der Verbotenen Stadt im Zentrum und dem Olympischen Park im Norden verläuft.

Von dieser Prämisse ausgehend, versucht das Gebäude, einen Mikrokosmos der umgebenden Stadtstruktur in einem Gebäude zu erschaffen – eine auf das Verlagswesen konzentrierte „MicroCity". Das bestehende homogene, streng unterteilte Bürogebäude wurde in eine heterogene Mischung miteinander verwobener Räume verwandelt, die zum Arbeiten, Lernen, aber auch für Einzelhandel und Freizeit genutzt werden können. In ein geschlossenes Gebäude wurde öffentlicher und gemeinschaftlicher Raum integriert; vertikale Kommunikationsachsen verbinden die aufgebrochenen Ebenen, Außenbereiche verbinden die Nutzer mit der Stadt.

Eine Reihe auskragender Volumen verschiedener Größe erweitern die bestehenden Ebenen. Die Änderungen konzentrieren sich auf die Nord- und Westseiten, was die Verbindung der Ebenen bei minimaler Modifizierung der vorhandenen Betonstruktur ermöglicht und auch externe Terrassen entstehen lässt. In den neuen Räumen sind Verkehrs- und Gemeinschaftsflächen untergebracht, die sich vom Erdgeschoss bis zum Dach erstrecken und ein riesiges Fenster auf das Leben und die Bewegung im Gebäude von der verkehrsreichen sechsspurigen Ringstraße darstellen.

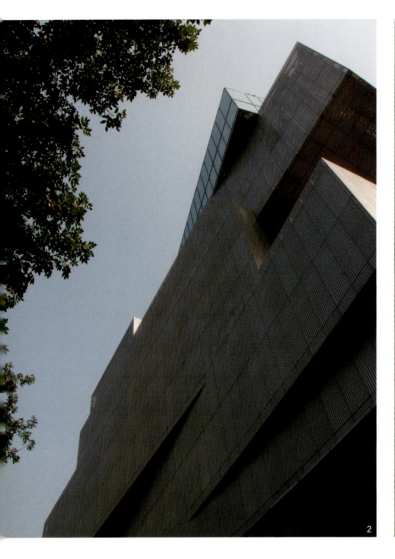

1 Exterior view Außenansicht
2 Part of west façade Teil der Westfassade
3 Exterior detail Fassadendetail
4 Elevation from west Westansicht
5 Ground floor plan Grundriss Erdgeschoss
6 First floor plan Grundriss 1. Obergeschoss
7 Sixth floor plan Grundriss 6. Obergeschoss
8 Tenth floor plan Grundriss 10. Obergeschoss

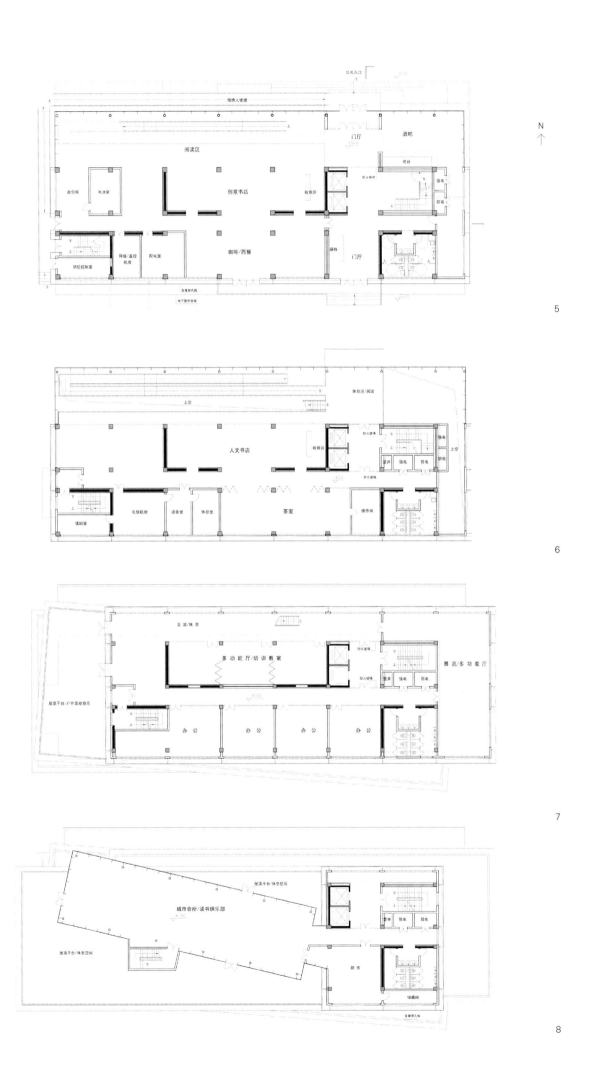

TM Studio
Room 1203, Unit 3
46 Lane Guokang Road
200092 Shanghai
Telephone +86 21 65 98 86 10
Fax +86 21 65 98 86 10
tmstudiosh@yahoo.com

TM Studio

TONG Ming
Established Gegründet
2000

Awards Preise

2006	Second Price of excellent Architectural Design, Jiangsu, China
2005	UNESCO Asia-Pacific Heritage Awards, Honorable Mention
2005	Second Price of excellent urban planning project of Shanghai

Important Projects Wichtige Projekte

2008	Zhou Chunya Art Studio, Shanghai
2007	Park Block Renovation, Luqiao Old Town, Taizhou
2006	Suquan Yuan, Shiquian Jie, Suzhou
2004	International Club of Hi-Tech District, Nanjing
2004	Dongs' House Tea House, Suzhou
2004	TM Studio workspace, Shanghai

22 Zhou Chunya Art Studio, Shanghai

Location Standort: Dayu village, Shanghai

Program Raumprogramm: Art studio Kunstatelier

Architectural team Architektenteam: TONG Ming, HUANG Xiaoying

Client Bauherr: ZHOU Chunya

Design Entwurf: 2008–2009

Construction Ausführung: 2008–2009

Site area Fläche Baugrundstück: 3,000 m²

Gross building area Bruttogeschossfläche: 1,460 m²

Photographer Fotograf: TM studio

Three sides of the project site are surrounded by rivers. The architects have used concrete structure and appearance to connect the building with the natural environment; the typical south-eastern country landscape, thus illustrating the quality and atmosphere of the artistic space.

The studio was divided into two parts to facilitate the working and living requirements of the artist, with careful consideration of the features of the site. One part is a new two-story building, designed as a private space in which the artist can work and relax. It is solid and exclusive to the outside to protect privacy. The other part is an existing lower traditional wooden frame building, which was preserved and used as a main axis around which to organize the layout of the newly developed area. Its courtyard system, representing a classical interpretation of space, serves the public activities of the artist.

Due to the height difference between the two parts, the roof of lower part became a beautiful terrace with an open view to the surrounding country landscape. The terrace was connected with the working and living spaces by various paths, expanding the public space of the ground floor and providing multiple usages as a result of different combinations with the other parts of the building. In order to adapt to the rainy season, the drainage system of the roof was designed in an open way and its detailing has been integrated into the structure of the skylight windows.

Das Grundstück für dieses Projekt wird auf drei Seiten von Flüssen eingerahmt. Die Architekten haben eine Betonstruktur und -ästhetik gewählt, um das Gebäude in Beziehung zu seiner Umgebung – der typischen Landschaft Südostchinas – zu setzen und somit die Qualität und Atmosphäre des Künstlerateliers zu unterstreichen.

Um den Arbeits- und Wohnansprüchen des Künstlers gerecht zu werden, wurde das Atelier unter genauer Berücksichtigung der Charakteristika des Ortes in zwei Teile geteilt. Der eine Teil ist der zweistöckige Neubau, der als privater Bereich geplant wurde, in dem der Künstler arbeiten und sich entspannen kann. Zum Schutz der Privatsphäre ist er massiv und nach außen abweisend. Der andere Teil ist ein bestehendes Fachwerkhaus, das erhalten wurde und die Hauptachse für die Grundrissorganisation des Neubaubereiches bildet. Sein Hofschema dient – als klassische Rauminterpretation – den gesellschaftlichen Aktivitäten des Künstlers.

Aufgrund des Höhenunterschieds zwischen den beiden Teilen wurde das Dach des niedrigeren Flügels zu einer schönen Terrasse mit Ausblick auf die umgebende Landschaft. Die Terrasse ist über mehrere Wege mit den Wohn- und Arbeitsbereichen verbunden, erweitert damit den öffentlichen Bereich des Erdgeschosses und steht durch die Kombination der verschiedenen Gebäudeteile unterschiedlichen Nutzungen offen. Als Referenz an die Regenzeit wurde das Entwässerungssystem des Daches offen gestaltet und auf Detailebene in die Struktur der Oberlichter integriert.

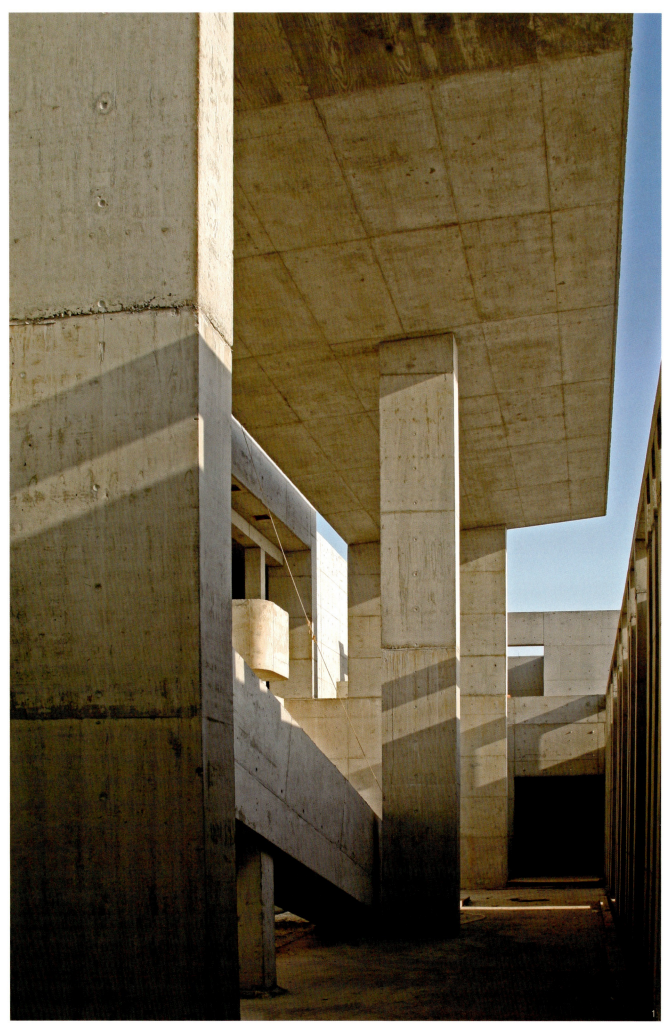

1	Courtyard Innenhof
2	North-east façade Nordostfassade
3	Roof Dach
4	Main stairs Haupttreppe
5	Exposed concrete surfaces Sichtbetonflächen
6	Site plan Lageplan

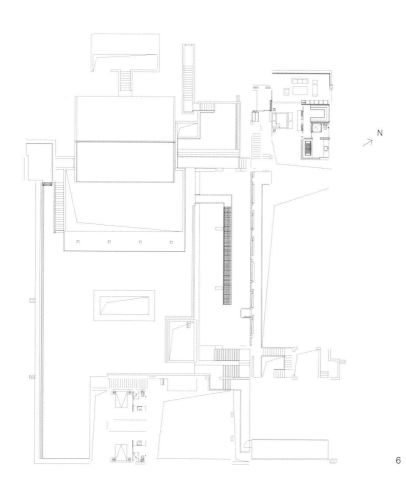

23 Park Block Renovation, Luqiao Old Town, Taizhou

Location Standort: Taizhou, Zhejiang

Program Raumprogramm: Residential, commercial, mixed Wohnen, Geschäfte, gemischte Nutzung

Architect Architekt: TONG Ming

Client Bauherr: Local Government Bezirksregierung

Design Entwurf: 2002–2005

Construction Ausführung: 2007

Site area Fläche Baugrundstück: 18,207 m²

Gross building area Bruttogeschossfläche: 10,500 m²

Photographer Fotograf: LV Hengzhong

Park Block is located on the eastern end of a four-kilometer-long historical street. There is a city park to the south and a busy shopping street to the north, making this block a junction area with multifold intentions.

Park Block comprises five buildings. The purpose of the design is to make connections through the different fabrics and scales of the surrounding environment, and to use local spatial order and surface texture to visualize overlapping layers. The patterned windows, reticulating walls, wedge-shaped openings and window panes, which are made in various materials and scales, could be produced in their own ways, however they overlap to form two or more figurations. They can interpenetrate without optically destroying each other.

This kind of chaos, the chief characteristic of this town, is a response to the principle, which dominates the generation of the town. Although each section develops individually and logically, they are visually integrated into a whole. This results in a kind of continuous movement, presenting the quality of complexity, and evoking the spatial atmosphere of a traditional townscape.

Meanwhile, this strategy will make construction much easier within an uncontrollable long-term project. The elegance of materials, details, joints, colors will no longer be important. Everything will happen automatically, and the results will be unexpected. In some way, this project attempts to simulate the logic and method of the construction of a city.

Der Park Block liegt am östlichen Ende einer vier Kilometer langen historischen Straße. Im Süden liegen ein Stadtpark und im Norden eine geschäftige Einkaufsstraße, welche diesen Block zu einem Kreuzungspunkt verschiedenster Aktivitäten machen.

Der Park Block umfasst fünf Gebäude. Die Intention des Entwurfes ist die Verbindung der verschiedenen Strukturen und Maßstäbe der Umgebung unter Verwendung räumlicher und baulicher Texturen, um die sich überlagernden Schichten zu artikulieren. Die Muster vor den Fenstern, die netzartig durchbrochenen Wände, keilförmigen Öffnungen und Fenster, die in verschiedenen Materialien und Maßstäben ausgeführt sind, könnten auch als selbständige Elemente stehen – sie überlagern sich aber und bilden dabei doppelte oder mehrfache Figuren. Sie durchdringen sich, ohne sich gegenseitig optisch zu zerstören.

Diese Art von Chaos – das Hauptmerkmal dieser Stadt – ist eine Reaktion auf die Prinzipien der Stadtentwicklung. Obwohl sich jeder Teil individuell und logisch entwickelt, bilden die Teile zusammen ein visuelles Ganzes. Alles ist ständig in Bewegung, dadurch entsteht Komplexität, die an die räumliche Qualität einer traditionellen Stadtstruktur gemahnt.

Diese Strategie wird das Bauen in einem solch unkontrollierbaren Langzeitprojekt sehr erleichtern. Die Eleganz der Materialien, Details, Verbindungen und Farben wird nicht mehr wichtig sein. Alles wird von selbst geschehen und zu unerwarteten Ergebnissen führen. Auf eine gewisse Art versucht das Projekt, die Logik und Methodik des Städtebaus zu simulieren.

1 View along street
Straßenansicht
2 Ground floor plan
Grundriss Erdgeschoss

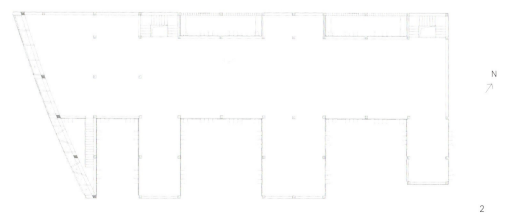

3 Façade change at street corner
  Fassadenwechsel an Straßenecke
4 Courtyard Innenhof
5 View of backside
  Rückwärtige Ansicht
6 Sections Schnitte

150 TM Studio

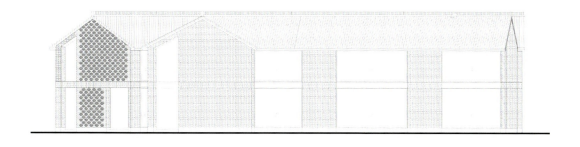

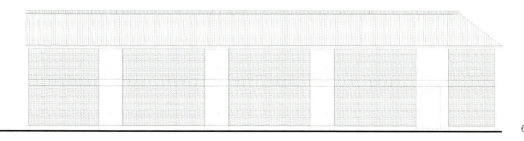

152　TM Studio

| 7, 8 | Courtyard with pond
Innenhof mit Teich |
| 9 | Alley Gang |
| 10 | Interior view Innenansicht |
| 11 | Elevations, section
Ansichten, Schnitt |

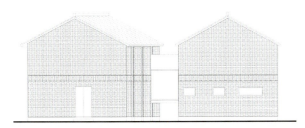
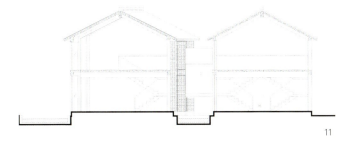
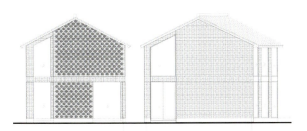

24 Suquan Yuan, Shiquan Jie, Suzhou

Location Standort: Suzhou, Jiangsu

Program Raumprogramm: Restaurant

Architect Architekt: TONG Ming

Client Bauherr: Zhongcheng Real Estate Development, Suzhou

Design Entwurf: 2004–2006

Construction Ausführung: 2005–2007

Site area Fläche Baugrundstück: 8,511 m²

Gross building area Bruttogeschossfläche: 5,613 m²

Photographer Fotograf: LV Hengzhong

Suquan Yuan is a redevelopment project intended to turn a huge parking space, which previously served a tourism company, into shopping and resort areas.

There were two challenges for this project: the first is its bottleneck entrance, which is only six meters wide in contrast to the large compound inside. Although it used to be quite appropriate for safeguarding and management reasons, it would be very disadvantageous for a commercial space to be segregated from the street front.

The other uncertainty of the project is usage. Like most speculative developments, it was almost impossible to anticipate the final user or definite functional purposes of the building during the design process.

As far as identity and expression are concerned, nothing could be better than a building as an impressive sign or a lively scene for the whole site. Based on the impressions and memories of local traditional architecture, the entrance club, which is intended to be a coffee shop, has been designed as a dark-brick box with an inserted wooden box, whose long windows can be opened and closed according to interior needs.

It is a pure box of light and shadows, materials and patterns. The structure is a simple-to-follow DOMINO diagram; the spaces inside are distinguished into a served area and servant rooms. The box could also accommodate further uncertain users; a stage that anticipates the occupation of future events.

Im Rahmen dieses Sanierungsprojekts sollten auf einem riesigen Parkplatz, der zuvor einem Tourismusunternehmen diente, Einkaufs- und Erholungsmöglichkeiten geschaffen werden.

Dabei gab es zwei Herausforderungen: zum einen den mit nur sechs Metern Breite im Verhältnis zur Größe des restlichen Grundstücks verengten Eingang. Diese Abtrennung von der Straße, die für einen Parkplatz aus Sicherheits- und Managementgründen angemessen war, ist für einen Einkaufsbereich sehr nachteilig.

Die andere Unwägbarkeit des Projektes ist die Nutzung. Wie bei den meisten spekulativen Entwicklungen war es fast unmöglich, die Endnutzer oder die letztendliche funktionelle Nutzung des Gebäudes während des Entwurfsprozesses vorauszuahnen.

Um dem Projekt Identität zu verleihen und Aufmerksamkeit zu erzeugen, erschien ein beeindruckendes, zeichenhaftes Gebäude oder eine lebendige Szenerie für das gesamte Grundstück am besten geeignet. In Anlehnung an lokale Architekturtraditionen ist der Klub am Eingang, der auch als Café dienen soll, als Holzkiste innerhalb einer dunklen Mauerwerkskiste entworfen worden, deren hohe Fenster je nach Bedarf geöffnet und geschlossen werden können.

Das Gebäude ist ein abstraktes Volumen aus Licht und Schatten, Materialien und Texturen: es hat eine einfach zu lesende „Dominostruktur". Das Innere ist in den Gastraum und Funktionsräume eingeteilt. Die Kiste könnte auch andere, nicht absehbare Nutzer aufnehmen und bietet nur den flexiblen Rahmen für zukünftige Nutzungen.

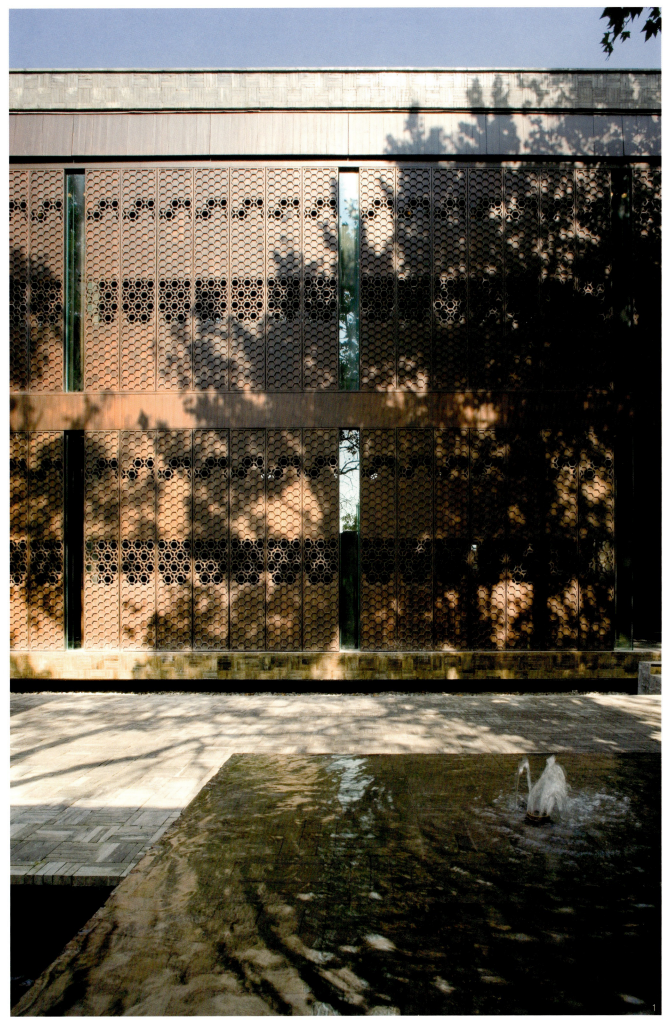

1	West façade Westfassade
2	North-west corner of façade Nordwest-Ecke der Außenfassade
3	Terrace on first floor Terrasse im 1. Obergeschoss
4, 5	Interior views Innenansichten
6	Ground floor plan Grundriss Erdgeschoss
7	First floor plan Grundriss 1. Obergeschoss

4

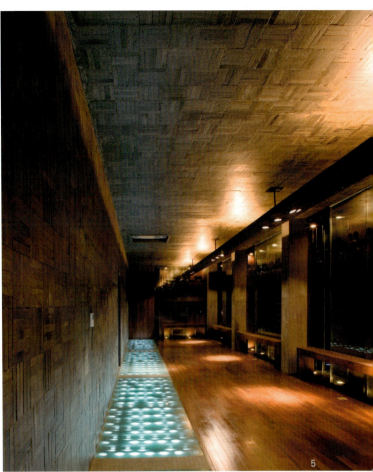
5

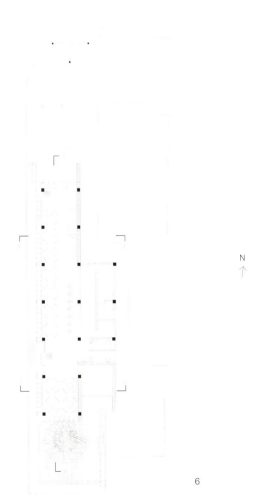
6

7

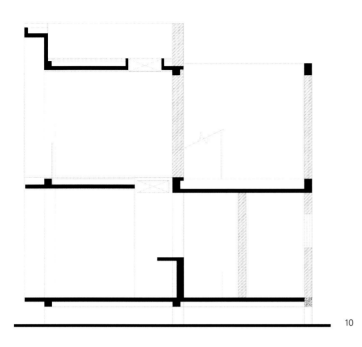
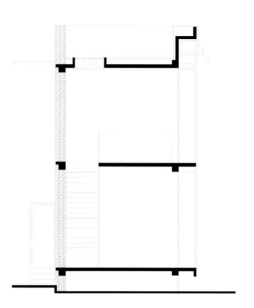

8, 9 Interior views Innenansichten
10, 11 Sections Schnitte
12 Elevation from north
Nordfassade

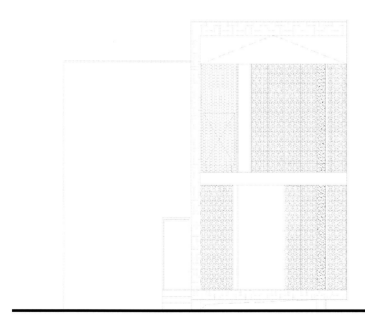

This publication coincides with the exhibition of the same name at Deutsches Architekturmuseum (DAM), from 29th August to 1st November 2009.
Diese Publikation erscheint anlässlich der gleichnamigen Ausstellung im Deutschen Architekturmuseum (DAM) vom 29. August 2009 bis 1. November 2009.

Organisation: General Administration of Press and Publication of the People's Republic of China
Partners Partner: Deutsches Architekturmuseum (DAM), China National Publications Import & Export (Group) Corporation, Liaoning Science and Technology Publishing Houses Co. Ltd.

© 2009 by jovis Verlag GmbH
First published by Liaoning Science and Technology Publishing House 2009.
Texts by kind permission of the authors. Pictures by kind permission of the photographers/holders of the picture rights.
Das Copyright für die Texte liegt bei den Autoren. Das Copyright für die Abbildungen liegt bei den Fotografen/Inhabern der Bildrechte.
All rights reserved. Alle Rechte vorbehalten.
Cover image (Endpaper) Coverfoto (Vorsatz): Amateur Architecture Studio: Ningbo History Museum, Photograph by Fotografie: LY Hengzhong
Translation English–German Übersetzung Englisch–Deutsch: Jörn Frenzel, Berlin
Translation German–English Übersetzung Deutsch–Englisch: Jeremy Gaines, Frankfurt/Main
English proofreading Englische Korrektur: Rachel Hill, Berlin
Design and layout Gestaltung und Layout: Ju Hai, Shenyang
Cover and endpaper design Umschlag- und Vorsatzgestaltung: Susanne Rösler, Berlin
Setting Satz: Vincent Illner, Berlin
Printing and binding Druck und Bindung: SNP Leefung Printers Ltd, Shen Zhen

Bibliographic information published by Die Deutsche Bibliothek
Die Deutsche Bibliothek lists this publication in the Deutsche Nationalbibliografie; detailed bibliographic data are available on the Internet at http://dnb.ddb.de
Bibliografische Information der Deutschen Bibliothek
Die Deutsche Bibliothek verzeichnet diese Publikation in der Deutschen Nationalbibliografie; detaillierte bibliografische Daten sind im Internet über http://dnb.ddb.de abrufbar.

jovis Verlag GmbH
Kurfürstenstraße 15/16
10785 Berlin

www.jovis.de

ISBN 978-3-86859-025-8